Teaching Emerging Scientists

Teaching Emerging Scientists

Fostering Scientific Inquiry with Diverse Learners in Grades K–2

Pamela Fraser-Abder, Ph.D.

New York University

Boston   Columbus   Indianapolis   New York   San Francisco   Upper Saddle River
Amsterdam   Cape Town   Dubai   London   Madrid   Milan   Munich   Paris   Montreal   Toronto
Delhi   Mexico City   Sao Paulo   Sydney   Hong Kong   Seoul   Singapore   Taipei   Tokyo

Acquisitions Editor: Kelly Villella Canton
Editorial Assistant: Annalea Manalili
Vice President, Director of Marketing: Quinn Perkson
Marketing Manager: Danae April
Production Editor: Janet Domingo
Editorial Production Service: Kathy Smith
Composition Buyer: Linda Cox
Manufacturing Buyer: Megan Cochran
Electronic Composition: Schneck-DePippo Graphics
Interior Design: Deborah Schneck

For related titles and support materials, visit our online catalog at www.pearsonpd.com.

Between the time website information is gathered and then published, it is not unusual for some sites to have closed. Also, the transcription of URLs can result in typographical errors. The publisher would appreciate notification where these errors occur so that they may be corrected in subsequent editions.

Printed in the United States of America

10 9 8 7 6 5 4 3 2 1   14 13 12 11 10

www.pearsonpd.com

ISBN-10: 0-205-56955-2
ISBN-13: 978-0-205-56955-7

To: Nicolas, Gabriel, and Alexander,
who keep me focused on seeing science through
the eyes of young children.

Contents

Chapter

Factors That Influence Your Science Teaching Philosophy   1

Chapter 2

How Young Children Learn and Think about Science   19

Chapter 3

Your Children and Science Learning 35

Chapter 4

The Inquiry Approach to Teaching and Learning Science 49

Chapter 5

Exploring Process Skills   61

Chapter 6

Establishing Your Science Program   83

Chapter

Chapter 8

Appendix 1

The National Science Education Standards and Benchmarks for Science Literacy   143

Appendix 2

Science Content Information for Grades K–2   159

Acknowledgments

I gratefully acknowledge the support of my colleagues: Robert Wallace, whose lessons, photos, and artwork appear in the book; Preeti Gupta and Frank Signorelli from New York Hall of Science, who share one of their professional development workshops; my graduate students Lindsay MacPherson, Audrey Elias, Hallie Saltz, and Lindsey Webster, now elementary teachers in New York City, who share their lessons and research project conducted during my graduate elementary methods course; and Kara Naidoo, a science teacher and doctoral student, who reviewed the science content in the Appendix. Caitlyn Herman and Tammy Lam provided valuable research and editorial assistance; my daughters Roxanne, Stacy, and Camilla were always available for editorial research and technological assistance. Janice Koch served as my support system as I began to envision the evolution of this book. My colleagues Jason Bloustein, Catherine Milne, Cecily Selby, and Marion Zachowski provided invaluable support.

Thanks to my reviewers: Jamie Barnett, Cherokee County Schools; Pascale Creek Pinner, Hilo Intermediate School; Anita R. O'Neill, Montgomery County Public Schools; Beverly Ramsey, Bobby Ray Memorial Elementary School; Scott D. Richman, Hillsborough County Public Schools; Nancy B. Smoot, Clemmons Elementary School; and Dawn Renee Wilcox, Spotsylvania County Schools. I also acknowledge the thousands of teachers and teacher educators with whom I have worked both locally and globally. Much of what I have written here is a reflection of what I have learned from you in our discussions and workshop activities.

Thank you.

Foreword

Classrooms are busy places and the demands on elementary school teachers are greater than ever before. As you go about your school day, the challenge to create community in your classrooms, attend to the business of the school day, and organize the mandated lessons surrounding language arts and mathematics often leaves little time to help students learn about the natural world by doing science with them.

This book is a wonderful way to make friends with science and, as a classroom teacher, engage your students in experiences and experiments that examine enduring concepts in science and that will engage you in conversations with them about what worked and what didn't work.

As a science teacher educator, I have worked extensively with Pamela Fraser-Abder and I know that the topics and lessons she designed for the practicing teacher will help you feel excited and inspired about teaching science to young children.

This book will facilitate your own and your students' science learning. From classroom-based experiments to using the resources in your environment, the activities in this book will help you implement science in your own classroom. Doing science with children means you will engage them in their own experiences and in their own thinking. Young children will gain practice making observations, manipulating materials, gathering information, and discussing their ideas.

During the early years, our students are natural explorers. Be sure to use the suggestions in each chapter to help you encourage their quest to understand "why" things happen. While *inquiry* is a term often used in school science, be sure to examine just what we mean by inquiry when we engage children in science activities. Establishing a science program in the early grades can be overwhelming. Be certain to use the suggestions in Chapter 6 to guide you in the development of early childhood science curriculum.

Finally, use this book as a tool to help you and your young students have fun while learning about the natural world.

Janice Koch

Preface

Dear Teacher of Emerging Scientists,

This book is written to assist you in developing, implementing, and evaluating your science teaching and your students' science learning. The research on science education and equity and professional development that I have conducted for over two decades provides the foundation for this research-based, yet practical and user-friendly, book. The title was chosen as a call to action to you, teachers of young children in kindergarten through grade 2, as you guide them on their journey into science during these crucial years. Like the flower they are now emerging as scientists.

As teachers, you play an important role in facilitating the learning process as your K–2 children begin their journey to scientific literacy. To better explore your critical role in the development of emergent scientists, you are encouraged to reflect on the following questions throughout the book:

- What am I teaching?

- Why am I teaching it?

- How am I teaching it?

- How do I know what my children have learned?

As you read this book you need to wear two hats: that of a learner and that of a teacher. You practice doing science through the activities and reflecting on what and how you are learning. Then you learn to step back and view your experience as a teacher. What ideas did you struggle with? What helped you in the struggle? What ideas are your children likely to struggle with? How can you help them in their struggle? What strategies can you use to help them as they develop their own understanding?

Although some school districts' intense focus on literacy development has resulted in less attention to science teaching and learning, teachers will now be required to teach science, which will be included in the state's accountability system. Given this new focus on teaching science, you may feel daunted, confused and maybe a little frightened. You might be asking yourself questions like: What do I need to know? What supplies do I need to purchase? Where can I find effective activities?

Some of you may already teach science and enjoy it. But others may find it a challenge to make the transition from teaching little or no science to having to teach science to your K–2 classes. This book is written to help you meet that challenge.

As you complete the reflections in this book, you will explore, through your science autobiography and other reflection opportunities, your personal traits that determine the what, why, and how you teach; your deep-seated, often unconscious feelings toward science teaching and learning; and your views on who has ownership of science. This approach to personal exploration is rooted in the context of schooling:

- What were your experiences with science as a student?
- What does it mean to teach science for all, and how do you teach for scientific literacy?
- What do you understand about how young children learn science?
- What are the implications of science in the daily lives of your children?

Begin to conceptualize science teaching as a personal activity that requires a large capacity for reflective thought and deliberate action and experimentation. This book provides both knowledge about science content and process, curriculum, instruction, and pedagogy as well as a venue for personal examination so that you may leave this professional development experience as a confident elementary teacher of science.

As you focus on teaching science, you will no doubt find numerous books written about methods of teaching elementary science. My goal is not to recreate these books but to share practical strategies with you and point you in the direction of potential activities and resources for use in your classroom and to help you expose your children to the informal world of science and to the surrounding community, which contains numerous, often free, resources for teaching science. Spend some time revisiting the experiences you had in your science methods courses and reviewing the texts you used as you engage in the activities in this book. The young children in your classroom are still filled with excitement and curiosity about nature. Let us use this to enhance their science learning. Many of the activities in this book deal with answering the questions your children might generate from interaction with their natural surroundings, whether urban, suburban, or rural. Let us involve our young children in activities that they will always remember and build on as they move to the upper elementary grades.

Our schools continue to cater to the needs of an increasingly diverse population. Diversity in learning styles and abilities, ethnicities, social class, religion, gender, culture, and language is represented in most of our schools. This book helps you to examine diversity in your classroom and determine how you can foster an effective learning community in your science classroom while being sensitive to the needs of all members of the class. Those of you who are teaching in the urban setting are well aware of the increasing diversity in your classrooms. For those of you teaching in suburban and rural settings, demographic changes are taking shape quickly. You will soon find yourself teaching an increasingly diverse student population. I invite you to do some in-depth reflection on who you are and who your children are. Before you can begin to teach science effectively you need to understand yourself and your teaching philosophy. Then you need to begin to develop an understanding of your children. You cannot teach unless you know your audience. What are their views of science and scientists? What prior knowledge do they bring to your classroom? What are the demographics of the community in which you teach? What kind of support can you reasonably expect from parents and the community? What are the implications of the diversity in your class for how you develop and teach science lessons?

This book incorporates the following practical strategies for in-service teachers:

- tips for urban teachers
- classroom management tips for teachers conducting inquiry lessons
- suggestions for teaching science to English language learners and children with special needs
- ideas for connecting science and other content areas
- suggestions for using informal resources to teach science
- ideas for connecting your emerging scientists with their local environment
- ideas for developing lessons based on the national and state science standards.

Good science teaching and learning is a result of meaningful preparation and collaboration among teachers, children, parents, and the community. As a teacher, you have the power to make an outstanding contribution to the scientific pipeline by nurturing the critical thinking skills of the emerging scientists in your classroom so they have the opportunity and foundation to become scientifically literate and our nation's future scientists.

My goal is to provide you with the information and prompts to help you evolve into an outstanding teacher of emerging scientists. This book would be considered a success if by the end of the second grade, your children maintain their curiosity and deep interest in science and continue to view science as a way of looking at and interacting with the world.

Let's begin our journey to scientific literacy!

1

Factors That Influence Your Science Teaching Philosophy

Focus Questions

- Why teach science to young children?
- Who are you, and how do you feel about science?
- What are your views of science and scientists?
- Who are your students?
- How can you help your students succeed in science?

The increasing number of children from diverse cultures entering U.S. schools, combined with the national goal of scientific literacy for all children creates a major dilemma for teachers who belong to cultures that are very different from the immigrant cultures. The emerging body of literature suggests that children from different cultures bring alternative ways of knowing, communicating, and experiencing the world, which may be incompatible with the way science is traditionally defined and taught in our schools and addressed in the state and national standards. This book begins by examining equity and access issues that have a major impact on science teaching and learning. During this in-depth investigation and reflection, you will examine the following two student-focused questions:

- Who are your children?
- What are their lives like?

Concurrent with this process of discovery about your children, you will also engage in an in-depth self examination and reflection of yourself and your often subconscious expectations for all children. The final self-reflection leads you to examine the question:

- How does knowing who you are and who your children are make you a better teacher?

Once you come to a better understanding about who you are and what culturally embedded issues your children bring to the classroom, you can move on to dealing with your scientific self and examine your views of science and scientists.

Throughout this book, you will find many reflective activities and be guided to collect many resources. Keep your reflections or entries in this book or in a journal, and file any research that you do online in a folder that you can use for reference in your curriculum planning and development.

Why Teach Science to Young Children?

Teacher Activity: Initial Reflection

List three reasons why you should teach science to children.

1. _____

   _____

2. _____

   _____

3. _____

   _____

As we enter the era of global warming, decreased food supplies and increased cost of energy, we become more aware of the importance of science and technology and the need to have our population capable of making decisions informed by scientific knowledge. At the same time, there is compelling evidence that only a small percentage of the children who pass through the school system develop any useful scientific literacy. We continue to produce graduates who lack even a basic understanding of science and technology, who have a negative attitude toward science, and who have not fully developed critical thinking skills capability. This paucity in science knowledge has increasingly unfortunate personal, social, and economic consequences, including the inability to take pleasure from the natural world, to make decisions that contribute to the sustainability of our environment, and to use science to inform decision-making processes. The increasing technological sophistication of the work place will require at least a basic knowledge and skill in science, mathematics, and technology.

Personal and civic decisions are often better made if guided by scientific knowledge. For example:

- When states propose shipping their garbage to other states or to remote areas in the state, can residents offer a better alternative?

- As new diet fads wax and wane, how do people sort out the competing claims and choose a safe method of losing weight?
- As the cost of gasoline rises each day and energy consumption becomes more and more of an economic issue, how do people respond? What knowledge do they use to guide their decisions?

Scientific understanding alone may not suffice to guide such decisions, but its absence will likely lead to poor solutions.

In the past it was believed that only a handful of smart children had the capacity to learn science while the remaining children—those who are average, and especially those who are poor, female, or in a minority group—are widely assumed to be incapable of learning the math required in science, too concrete of mind to grasp scientific abstractions, unwilling to endure the rigors of science education or do not have the necessary parental support and guidance.

There is ample evidence, however, that the problem is not the child, but instead that science is not being taught or is often taught in a way that progressively diminishes children's interest in the subject and their confidence in their capacity to learn it. For many years, most elementary schools have taught only two subjects seriously—reading and mathematics—on the flawed assumption that this allows them to "leave no child behind."

Even where children are also taught science, the nature of the content and the way it is presented often fail to engage young children's minds. Some young children are taught science as a series of fun experiments; some are engaged in kit-based science. Others are offered "textbook" science, where they are taught facts and concepts but are not given enough time and experience to connect those facts with the realities of the natural world or to grasp the underlying principles that make sense of it all. Thus, children can quickly become bored by the seemingly pointless memorization of content. This type of teaching causes many of our elementary children to be turned off by science. Not surprisingly, many children from all social classes and ethnic backgrounds decide that science is boring and too hard. All children are capable of learning science and should have the opportunity to do so. Science provides them with a foundation for life as critical thinking adults who can contribute to the well-being of themselves and society.

When we consider the question "Why teach science?" it seems easy to answer in terms of the importance of science in society. We can immediately see the multitude of benefits from scientists' research and technologists' application in medicine, industry, transportation, agriculture, electronics, and technology. Think about what your day would be like if all of the scientific advances and applications that have been made in your lifetime alone were suddenly erased. How very different life would be without television, cell phones, or computers! You need to prepare your young children for a life full of technology, a type of life which has not yet been envisioned. You need to provide them with the skills to exist in that new world—a world in which critical thinkers and problem solvers will be the ones who survive and live successful lives.

The development of critical thinking skills has been emphasized as being of major importance if we want to produce rational thinkers and decision makers who can contribute to society. Great scientists are critical thinkers. The skills practiced by scientists help children become critical thinkers. Critical thinkers

- continually seek to know and to understand
- question all things
- interpret all available data
- base judgment on evidence
- respect logic
- consider consequences of their actions
- demonstrate intellectual independence

These critical life skills should be taught as part of science. For young children, their entire world is their laboratory; they continually seek to know, understand, and question all things. Though their efforts are often fumbling, children readily search for data and want verification. But what happens to their spirit of inquiry as they progress up the educational ladder? Why does the number of questions decrease? Perhaps part of the reason is a lack of opportunity to use scientific process thinking skills or critical thinking skills.

There is no better way to help children satisfy their wanting to know, their questioning and searching, than to allow them to interact with objects and events of the natural world. This is what is involved in their doing science, why it is so important to them, and why you should make it important in your teaching. As a teacher of young children, your major role is to foster and encourage this questioning, this unending curiosity.

Children come to school with a constant need to investigate everything they encounter, but by the end of the third grade this deep interest in science sometimes fades from lack of nurturing on the part of teachers, parents and the community. Our young children, our emerging scientists, only achieve their potential if they receive a high-quality science education. And you hold the key.

Teacher Activity: Why Teach Science to Young Children?

Now that you have read and reflected on the above, give five reasons why you think you should teach science to young children.

1. _____

   _____

2. _____

   _____

3. _____

   _____

4. _____

   _____

5. _____

   _____

Now that you have reflected on why you should teach science, let us turn to figuring out who you are and why you teach as you do.

Your Personal Context

Who Are You, and How Do You Feel about Science?

In a recent survey conducted as part of their classroom observation, some of my graduate students examined the status of elementary science teaching in the schools in which they were currently student teaching. Their results lent support to the belief that they do not need to teach science when they have their own elementary classroom. Their results showed that 40 percent of classes had a cluster teacher who was responsible for teaching one to two science sessions per week, 25 percent of classes had teachers who did one to three science sessions per week, while 35 percent of classrooms had no science instruction. These kinds of results indicate that many teachers may be struggling with understanding that the classroom teacher must teach science as an essential part of a well-rounded education that prepares children to be critical thinkers, problem solvers, and informed decision makers. These results mirror what is currently happening in elementary schools as teachers focus their teaching primarily on mathematics and reading. With the introduction of No Child Left Behind, elementary teachers have had to focus their attention on mathematics and reading, the subjects that were being tested. However, with the recent introduction of science testing, more attempts are now being made to teach science in the classroom. To begin your journey of effective science teaching, you need to start with a clear idea as to where you position yourself in science teaching.

Teacher Activity: Initial Self-Reflection

Reflecting on the following questions will help you begin to focus on your science teaching. Be honest with your responses. No one will see the answers.

1. Can you recall what made you decide to teach young children?

_____

_____

_____

2. What did you think of science then? Did you think it would be a difficult subject to teach?

_____

_____

3. How often are you teaching science now?

_____

_____

4. How are you teaching it? What strategies and resources do you use?

_____

_____

_____

- What is the status of your current science teaching?
- Are you the classroom teacher who teaches science as part of your daily curriculum?
- Do you work closely with a cluster teacher, integrating what you do with what is being covered in science?
- Do you leave all the science teaching up to the cluster teacher?

The answers to these questions will determine how much preparation you need to do to plan for teaching your emerging scientist.

Let us begin this journey by reflecting on you and your in-depth feelings about science and science teaching.

Based on your self-reflection, you might find that you fall into one of these categories:

- did not like science and do not teach it
- loved science and love teaching it
- teaching K–2 because you enjoy teaching young children
- teaching science because you have to

Whatever category you fall into, the exercises in this book will help you develop into an effective teacher of K–2 science. It is important that as you prepare for teaching science, you come to terms with your science teaching philosophy.

The best teachers are the ones who can respect and cultivate individual differences in their students.

What Is Your Teaching and Learning Style?

Here are some questions you may ask and respond to in order to construct a useful picture of yourself as a teacher.

Teacher Activity: What's Your Teaching and Learning Style?

1. Do I plan for what might happen in my class ahead of time, or would I rather cope with problems as they arise?

_____

_____

2. Am I able to empower my students to do science even though I sometimes feel powerless myself?

_____

_____

3. Am I a visual, auditory, naturalistic, or kinesthetic learner/teacher?

_____

_____

4. Under which of Gardner's learning styles (see Table 1.1) would I find myself described?

_____

_____

5. Do I like objective testing tools made by an outside person, or would I rather rely on my classroom interaction to assess my children's learning?

_____

_____

6. Do I use differentiated instruction in my class?

_____

_____

7. Is my classroom teacher dominated or teacher facilitated?

_____

_____

Howard Gardner, in his Theory of Multiple Intelligences, identified eight different types of intelligence: bodily-kinesthetic, interpersonal, linguistic, logical-mathematical, intrapersonal, spatial, musical, and naturalistic. Table 1.1 (page 10) is a brief description of each intelligence based on Gardner's work.

Gardner points out that, in this nation, education usually focuses primarily on linguistic and logical-mathematical intelligence. Intelligence is a mixture of several abilities that are all of great value in life. But nobody is good at them all. In life, we meet people who collectively are good at different things. For further study, it is recommended that you read Gardner's books referenced at the end of this book. You should also visit this Website (http://usd.edu/~bwjames/tut/learning-style/stylest.html) and take a quick test to determine your learning style.

Table 1.1 Gardner's Multiple Intelligences

Intelligence	Description
Bodily-kinesthetic	People are generally adept at physical activities (movement and doing) such as sports and often prefer activities that utilize movement.
Interpersonal	This area has to do with interactions with others. People in this category are usually extroverts and are characterized by their sensitivity to others' moods, feelings, temperaments, and motivations and their ability to cooperate in order to work as part of a group.
Linguistic	People with verbal-linguistic intelligence display a facility with words and languages.
Logical–mathematical	These individuals excel at reasoning capabilities, abstract pattern recognition, scientific thinking and investigation, and the ability to perform complex calculations.
Intrapersonal	Those who are strongest in this intelligence are typically introverts, self-reflective, and prefer to work alone. They are usually highly self-aware and capable of understanding their own emotions, goals, and motivations.
Spatial	People with strong visual-spatial intelligence are typically very good at visualizing and mentally manipulating objects. They have a strong visual memory and are often artistically inclined.
Musical	Those who have a high level of musical-rhythmic intelligence display greater sensitivity to sounds, rhythms, tones, and music. They normally have good pitch, and may even have absolute pitch, and are able to sing, play musical instruments, and compose music.
Naturalistic	This intelligence involves the ability to understand and work effectively in the natural world. This is exemplified by biologists and zoologists.

Teacher Activity: Reflection

This reflection provides you with some understanding of your teaching and learning style. It helps you to understand your mindset as you prepare for science teaching and interactions with your students. You need to understand yourself and your teaching style before you can begin to develop plans for teaching your students.

1. Where do you see yourself represented in Gardner's Learning Style Inventory?

_____

_____

_____

2. How does knowledge of Gardner's multiple intelligence help you in teaching science?

_____

_____

_____

3. What are the implications for how you teach science?

_____

_____

_____

4. How does it affect how your students learn science?

_____

_____

_____

5. How will it affect your teaching strategies and lesson planning?

_____

_____

_____

What Are Your Views on Science and Scientists?

Teacher Activity: How Do You Define Science?

1. Science is . . .

_____

_____

2. Do you see science as a body of knowledge that has to be memorized? Why? Is this how you were exposed to science?

_____

_____

Teacher Activity: Draw a Scientist

Once you have come up with your own definition for science, draw what you think a scientist looks like:

Now consider these questions:

1. What are your thoughts on what scientists look like?
2. What does your drawing reflect?
3. Why do you think that this is your image of a scientist?
4. How many scientists do you know?
5. Do you have friends who are scientists?
6. Have you always avoided having scientists as friends?

During a recent professional development program, I asked teachers to submit anonymous drawings of scientists. Figure 1.1 shows some representations of selected drawings.

These drawings are rarely representative of scientists, although they do tend to perceive the world slightly differently from nonscientists. Scientists tend to try to find responses to the types of questions that your K–2 children are always asking. They are observant, curious, analytical, critical, and objective in their conclusions. In their work, they do not jump to conclusions without first verifying their facts. They constantly use the science process skills.

Figure 1.1   Teacher Drawings of Scientists

They are patient, knowing that often it takes a long time to find answers. These drawings represent a naïve view of a scientist; not all scientists work in a laboratory or wear lab coats.

What Were Your Early Experiences with Science?

Teacher Activity: Early Experiences with Science

Try to recall some of your earlier experiences with science as you rekindle some of your earlier childhood curiosity.

1. As a student, what were your experiences with science?

   _____

   _____

2. What was your experience with the natural world?

   _____

   _____

Teacher Activity: Write Your Science Autobiography

Think back as far as you can. Use these questions to write your science autobiography.

1. What do you recall about your first exposure to science?

   _____

   _____

2. Can you recall events from your K–2 classroom?

   _____

   _____

3. What are your earliest memories of science and your involvement in science, both in and out of school?

   _____

   _____

4. Are they good memories?

   _____

As you share your science autobiographies with others, you will see that we have all had varying experiences with science. We have learned from these experiences and want to create opportunities for memorable experiences with science for our K–2 emerging scientists.

What does this tell you about your views of science and scientists? Janice Koch (2005) aptly coined the expression "we teach who we are" in discussing science autobiographies. If we have negative stereotypes and perceptions of science and scientists, then that is what we teach our children. It is extremely important for you to closely examine your view toward science, scientists, and teaching science, because your perceptions and viewpoint will influence how you engage your children in science. Your feelings also impact your expectations and perceptions of children's ability and capacity to do science and become scientists. It is helpful to consider the following points in your approach to teaching science:

- Will your teaching reflect science as a static body of knowledge consisting of one right answer that has to be memorized or as a constantly expanding dynamic search for answers to questions that arise from our interaction with the natural world and our quest to better understand the world in which we live?

- Will you provide the kinds of experiences that will enable the scientist in each child to emerge?

- Will you enable your children to develop the dispositions that will allow them to continue on their journey to becoming scientifically literate?

Teacher Activity: Your Science Story

Think about your experience with science as a child and write your personal "science story."

1. What did you like?

_____

_____

2. What did you hate?

_____

_____

3. How much of it can you remember?

_____

You want your children to have good memories of their science class. You want them to be able to recall some of the questions they had and the process they used for finding answers to those questions.

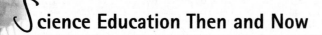

Science Education Then and Now

How has science education changed since the 1950s? Science education has changed dramatically since the launching of Sputnik by the Soviet Union in 1957. Today as we teach science to K–2 children:

- Student questions guide science activities.
- Children experience examples of concepts before their names are presented.
- Life, physical, and earth sciences are treated in a more balanced way.
- Reading, doing, and thinking about science are combined.
- Mathematics, social studies, and language arts are incorporated into science in a more comprehensive, multidisciplinary way.
- The process skills of science are used to design more meaningful conditions for learning.
- Science learning is recognized as an internalized long-term change in behavior.

To some of us, this is a completely new way of looking at science. It is not the way we were taught, and now, as we teach our emerging scientists, we need to undergo a paradigm shift in the way we view science teaching and learning.

Many of us who find science a difficult subject to teach fit under the broad category of "fear of venturing into the unknown." This hesitancy might also stem from a resistance to change in general. The more uncomfortable you are about doing something, the easier it is to procrastinate or avoid the task entirely. In addition, there may be personal phobias or biases to overcome, including fear of the vast amount of scientific knowledge that is now available. There is no denying that we are living in the midst of an explosion of knowledge that no other generation has ever experienced. We are now surrounded by nanotechnology, plastics, synthetics, numerous electronics devices, computers, lasers, iPods, and iPhones. It should come as no surprise that this explosion of knowledge, with its effects on technology, elicits fear in some and insecurity in others—and not just elementary teachers. But if you are willing, you can replace your feelings of fear and insecurity with new skills and knowledge. Additionally, teaching hands-on inquiry science requires far more preparation of physical materials than teaching other subjects. However, the time spent in the preparation is well worth the interest, participation, and achievement that you can foster in your young children.

Teacher Activity: Final Self-Reflection

Examine this question: How does knowing who you are and who your students are make you a more effective teacher?

_____

_____

_____

_____

_____

_____

_____

_____

Take-Away Thought

Before you can be an effective teacher, you must know who you are.

How Young Children Learn and Think about Science

Focus Questions

- Can you recall your first experience with science?

- What are your children's views of science and scientists?

- What does research say about how young children view science and scientists?

- What is science?

- What are K–2 children's ideas about science?

- How do young children learn science?

- What are some common misconceptions in your science classroom?

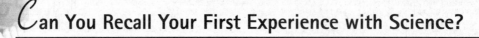

Can You Recall Your First Experience with Science?

Spend a few minutes going back in time to when you were a young child. Can you recall how the world appeared to you as a child? What did you think when at age 5 you saw your first caterpillar, your first flower, your first toy car? Can you remember what questions you had? Did you ever find answers to those questions?

One way of recreating your thinking as a five- or six-year-old is to do the following activities with a young child. Last summer, I took my five-year-old neighbor to the botanical gardens to see the butterflies. She was bubbling over with excitement to be going to the gardens, on the way there she wanted to know:

- What color are the butterflies?
- Can a butterfly fly from the gardens to my home? (a distance of 10 miles)

When we arrived, she was ecstatic to see the range of colors and shapes. Her questions flowed:

- Why does that one keep going back to the same plant?
- Do butterflies drink water?
- How can you tell what color butterfly will come from the caterpillar?
- Are all caterpillars green?

The questions were unending. It was wonderful to see butterflies through the eyes of a five-year-old. I had forgotten the excitement of my first sight of so many butterflies in one place.

Teacher Activity: Children's Questions I

Take a five-year-old on a nature walk. List the questions that arise.

_____

_____

_____

_____

(continued on next page)

Teacher Activity: Children's Questions I (continued)

_____

_____

_____

_____

_____

Teacher Activity: Children's Questions II

Bring a caterpillar to your K–2 classroom. Write down the questions that emerge from your children.

_____

_____

_____

_____

_____

_____

_____

_____

As you reflect on these experiences, do you find that there is a sense of excitement and curiosity in children's questions? They are not afraid to ask questions and want to find out about things you have never thought about, things you might not have connected to what they were doing or seeing. This never-ending sense of curiosity, of wanting to know more, is what you have to nurture in your children.

We should always encourage our children to ask questions. If we can't answer all of their questions, that's all right—no one has all the answers, even scientists. And children don't need lengthy, detailed answers to all of their questions. We can propose answers, test them out, and check them with someone else (with a scientist or online).

We can also encourage our children to tell us their ideas and listen to their explanations. Being listened to will help them to gain confidence in their thinking, develop their skills and interest in science, and improve their communication skills. Listening helps us to determine just what children know and don't know. It also helps children figure out what they know.

What Are Your Children's Views of Science and Scientists?

As young children interact with nature, they begin to emerge as scientists. They experience the joy of being a scientist and of discovering new facts, as they do science.

Kindergarten student visits a museum with dad.

*First grader doing a
dinosaur dig with dad.*

Second grader in nature.

Before you begin teaching science, ask your children "What is science?" Their
responses might surprise you. Here are some responses from an interview with
K–2 children:

- Science is growing when you look at seeds grow.
- Science is formulas—making things big and small.
- Science is drawing—looking at worms.
- Science is technology.

As I reflected on their responses, I began to realize that their responses
were informed by recent activities conducted during their last science class
and from listening to their friends, parents, and siblings talk about science.

Classroom Activity: What Is Science?

What responses does your class have for the question?

_____

_____

_____

_____

_____

_____

_____

_____

Once they have given you their definition of science, ask them to draw a scientist.

Classroom Activity: Children's Drawings of a Scientist

Give each child a sheet of paper and ask them to draw a scientist, providing as much detail as possible. Then consider these questions:

1. How do they picture a scientist?

_____

_____

2. Do their drawings reflect the stereotypical view of a scientist—bald or wild hair, male, glasses, pocket protector, lab coat, etc.?

_____

_____

What Does Research Say about How Young Children View Science and Scientists?

Barman and his colleagues (2000) conducted a variety of studies on children's views of science and scientists. (You will find a list of some of his studies in the references.) The results of one study indicated that most of the scientists that were depicted in the drawings by children were white males. Children in grades K–2 represented females in drawings more often (42 percent) than children in grades 3–5 (27 percent) and grades 6–8 (25 percent). When depicting the ethnic background of a scientist, 69 percent of grades K–2 children, 80 percent of grades 3–5 children and 74 percent of grades 6–8 children depicted the scientist as Caucasian. This study was conducted in 1999. Since then, there have been major attempts to develop scientific literacy in all our students.

Teacher Activity: Reflection

1. Do the drawings and definitions from your children mirror the research findings from the Barman study?

   _____

   _____

2. Do the definitions and drawings of your children mirror what you have been doing with them in your class?

   _____

   _____

3. Do you see a difference between the responses of students in the Barman study and your students?

   _____

   _____

4. What can you do to help your students develop a better understanding of science and scientists?

   _____

   _____

Remember that you are a significant role model for your children, and they often reflect what you say and do, often without your realizing it. If you subconsciously show them that you do not like science or think that scientists are weird, this is what they learn and what gets reflected in their drawings. As you begin to develop your teaching activities, think of strategies you can use to direct your young children away from the negative attitudes toward science and scientists demonstrated by the children in the Barman study. In your classroom, provide your children with examples showcasing female, minority, or outdoor scientists.

I invite you to assess your present abilities and attitudes toward science and science teaching. I encourage you to reflect on the ideas presented in this chapter. Once you come to a better understanding about who you are as a teacher and what culturally embedded ideas your children bring to the classroom, you can begin to focus on the pedagogical issues surrounding teaching emerging scientists.

When you decided to become a teacher, you might not have thought of yourself as a science teacher. It is my hope that in reading here about teaching science to K–2 children, you will see this as a journey of discovering strategies that you can use to help children on their pathway to true scientific literacy. As teachers, you need to understand science, the nature of science, and how young children learn science. You also need to develop appropriate instructional skills to help children become scientifically literate.

My work with many elementary teachers has taught me that before you can be confident in your ability to teach science, you need to develop

- a better understanding of science and scientists
- a better understanding of how K–2 children learn science
- appropriate science teaching strategies, resources, and materials
- a way to overcome fear or uncertainty about teaching science

What Is Science?

In a study of over 4,000 teachers, parents, children and scientists, subjects were asked to define the word *science* (Fraser-Abder, 2005). It was a daunting task to filter out of their responses a single and common definition of science. Let me share with you some of those definitions.

Science is . . .

- the constant search for answers about the universe around us
- the study of life and nature

- divided into many different areas: biology, chemistry, physics, etc.
- gathering data and then analyzing it
- the study of the world and how it all fits together
- experimentation
- the process of inquiry, the curiosity to explore, to solve problems, and verify information

As you can see from the examples above, there was a wide variation in responses across all respondents. However, as I examined the responses more closely, what emerged was one point of agreement—namely, the dual nature of science as content and process. *Science is an ongoing activity of exploration and the knowledge that comes out of that exploration.* That body of knowledge includes matter, energy, the organisms that inhabit the universe, and the interactions among these organisms and their environment. The exploration that involves observations, measurements, classification, hypotheses, predictions, and, finally, experimentation to verify discoveries and new findings becomes the basis for additional predictions and further explorations (see Figure 2.1 for the processes used in grades K–2). This unending journey where each answer leads to more questions represents the process

Figure 2.1   Science as the Study of the Interaction among Organisms and Their Environment

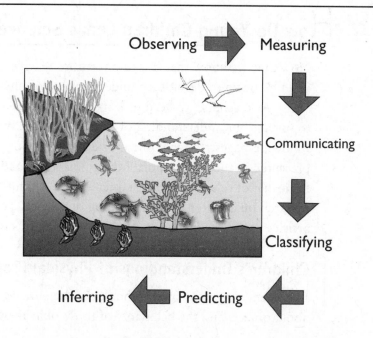

of science. *Scientists are involved in this constant exploration and search for the knowledge that comes from this exploration.* Each new exploration brings new questions and this is what makes science so interesting and engaging. Scientists are constantly asking Why? How? Where? What?

What Are K–2 Children's Ideas about Science?

Children develop their own ideas about the physical world, ideas that reflect their special perspectives. Below are some perceptions from some six-year-old children:

- At nighttime butterflies become moths.
- Some people can tell what time it is by looking at the sun, but I have never been able to make out the numbers on the sun.
- A blizzard is when it snows sideways.
- Worms "grow up" to become snakes.

Children's experiences help them form their ideas, and these often do not match current scientific interpretations. We need to allow our children to ask questions and make mistakes. With time and adequate experiences, children develop scientific understandings.

We can help our children look at things in new ways. For instance, in regard to the blizzard, we could ask: "Have you ever seen it snow sideways? What do you think causes it to move sideways sometimes?"

How Do Young Children Learn Science?

Now that we know that it is important to teach science. Let us look at how children begin to develop an understanding of physical, life, and earth sciences. As teachers, we need to learn from the research on child development to further our understanding of how children develop ideas in science. In the following pages, you will find a brief summary of a small part of the research presented in the 2006 report *Taking Science to School* (Duschl et al., 2006). In the list of references for Chapter 2, you will find numerous references to research on children's understanding of science. You will find these books or articles useful reading as you further explore this topic.

Children's Understandings of Physical Properties

Before entering elementary school, children are constantly refining their ideas about objects and the behaviors of those objects over intervals of time and space. By twelve months, children already have a rudimentary understanding of physical properties. At this same time, children are capable of making inferences as to the reasonable and unreasonable causes of the motion of inanimate objects.

Children also have a general knowledge of physical objects but an inability to use this knowledge in a wider range of tasks requiring planning or sequencing of actions. Children learn, however, through a process of trial and error. For example, a child, unlike most adults, would put an object on an unbalanced surface and learn from the consequences of the action the properties of the objects.

Though children do not have a vocabulary base or an understanding of the application of certain scientific concepts (such as trajectory), their actions reflect an understanding of how an object moves through space. For example, a child will adjust the angle and strength of the ball they are throwing to anticipate the trajectory. The concepts of force that children use to explain force in physical situations is intuitive.

Concepts in chemistry are foreign to most children before they enter elementary school. Children at the preschool level can distinguish differences in size. However, their conception of size is defined in terms of bigness without an understanding of spatial dimensions. Weight and density have yet to be differentiated as distinct properties of matter. Children's understandings of properties of matter undergo dramatic changes as they begin to understand measures of weight, volume, density, and material type.

Young children are also just beginning to develop concepts of matter that include both solids and liquids. Their understanding is initially grounded in commonsense perceptual properties—such as matter being something you can touch, feel, or see rather than something that has mass and takes up space. The misconception of matter translates into difficulties understanding that matter continues to exist when divided into tiny pieces unable to be seen with the naked eye.

Children's Understandings of Animals

Young students initially have no sense of the living and nonliving world and only think of living things as social beings. It is thought that children's misconceptions with living and nonliving things emerge because animals are understood as social agents with desires, goals, and other thinking and emotional states that explain their actions, whereas plants seem to lack these qualities. Based on psychological similarities to humans, children have a tendency to underattribute biological properties to simpler organisms in the plant and animal kingdom.

Young students are not aware of the mechanisms that underlie biological processes, such as digestion, movement, respiration, and reproduction. On one level children understand that organisms will physically deteriorate without food and that there is a transformation of food into essential components for use in the body. However, they do not understand that organic molecules release energy units that are used for the contraction of muscles and, subsequently, movement.

During elementary school, students show major growth in their understanding of the living world as they gain more facts and have more exposure to plants and animals through observations. Children become more aware of what plants and animals do, what their parts are and how those parts work, and what their insides look like—thus gaining a better understanding of structure and function. Though children do become more aware of the structure and function of plants and animals during elementary school, there are still many misconceptions at the cellular level of functioning and mechanics.

Children are quick to learn new concepts and fit those concepts within the existing conceptual framework. Children will learn that there can be different types of dogs, for instance, or that there are subtypes or new parts or properties of particular kinds of things. But because children already know that animals (such as dogs) can vary in size, body type, and eating preferences, children readily fit new information into the framework of their present knowledge. Subsequently, identifying new kinds of animals that have different clusters of attributes to the ones that children are already familiar with does not fundamentally change their understanding of the organism. Additionally, adding a new superordinate that unites subtypes of animals is not difficult when they are united by common properties that are easy to understand (i.e., learning that bears, dogs, and cats are all mammals).

Children's Understandings of Plants

One of the common misconceptions about plants is that plants are biological mechanisms emerging from the soil. Children do not understand the contribution of carbon dioxide in the developmental process.

As children learn that plants, like animals, are living things, misconceptions often result. Children have a tendency to think that plants behave just like animals and perform activities such as eating and sleeping. Children's misconceptions about the way plants eat are suggestive of the idea that their food is animate and comes from the soil rather than being synthesized during the process of photosynthesis from sugars in their leaves. Misconceptions about photosynthesis are attributed to children's difficulties in understanding matter. This limitation extends to a misconceived understanding of growth and decay.

Children's Understandings of Earth Science

Certain views of children's understandings of earth science suggest that preschool children develop a set of beliefs or framework theory that helps guide the emergence of culture-specific views. Children's understanding of the world translates into two basic facts: the world is flat, and objects that are unsupported fall down. As children learn more about cosmology and the Earth, they reinterpret their beliefs.

Research has shown that learning about Earth's spherical shape and gravity is a difficult concept for young students. It is not until fourth grade that students are able to better understand both the shape of the Earth as a sphere as well as the concept of gravity working as a force to pull objects towards the center of the Earth. In order for students to better understand the Earth and its forces, it means having a clarification of ideas, thinking through and understanding models, and applying their understandings and conceptual models to observable phenomena.

What Are Some Common Science Misconceptions in Your Classroom?

Teacher Activity: Misconceptions in Your Classroom

1. Can you remember some of your original misconceptions about Life, Physical, and Earth Science?

   _____

   _____

   _____

   _____

2. Reflect on the two activities earlier in this chapter. What misconceptions did you note while doing the activities?

   _____

   _____

   _____

   _____

A few years ago, Laura Henriques (2000) shared some of these misconceptions and ideas at a science teachers meeting. Table 2.1 has been adapted from her ideas.

Table 2.1 Children's Misconceptions and Teaching Ideas

Topic of Misconception	What Students Think	Ideas for Teaching
Worms	Worms help plants grow by getting rid of things that are bad for plants.	Study real worms in your classroom. By studying worms, students will not only learn about worms' role as decomposers, but will also study other important science standards involving animal characteristics and habitats.
Bees	Bees do specific things for the purpose of helping plants.	Organisms carry on activities for the purpose of their own health and survival and, in the process, also become important to other organisms. Do a role-playing pollination simulation with students with a focus on why the bee visits plants and what it does with the nectar it collects.
Soil	Soil provides a support structure and food for plants.	Provide examples of plants that grow in water without soil (e.g., aquariums). Have students germinate seeds in a moist environment without soil, in a nutrient-rich moist environment, without soil, and in moist soil. They will see that the plant germinates and begins to grow in each case, but does not grow as well without nutrients. They will also see that the stem grows upward and the roots downward.
Sunlight	Sunlight helps plants grow by keeping them warm.	Have students grow plants in a warm, lighted environment and compare this with plants grown in a warm, dark environment. Students will see that initially when plants germinate, both sets of plants will grow, but those in the dark are not as green. Over time, the plants in the dark die because, without light, they cannot produce their own food.
Trees and grass	Trees and grass are not plants.	Expose students to various plants by visiting a greenhouse or botanical garden. This will help them understand that there are non-flowering plants and plants that do not always have the typical plant parts that students associate with angiosperms.

As we talk about teaching science to young children, you will see this as a journey of reflections on strategies you can use to help students on their pathway to true scientific literacy. You need to understand science, the nature of science and how young children learn science if you are to help them become scientifically literate. You also need to develop appropriate instructional skills to help children become scientifically literate. The activities in this book will support you as you evolve into an outstanding teacher of emerging scientists.

Take-Away Thought

Science is an ongoing activity of exploration and the knowledge that comes out of that exploration. Science is process and content.

Your Children and Science Learning

Focus Questions

- Who are your children?
- What are your class' demographics?
- How can you develop a cultural understanding of your children?
- How can you use your children's lived experiences to inform your science teaching?
- What are your expectations for your children?
- How can you help your K–2 children succeed in science?

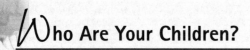

Who Are Your Children?

Let's reflect on two important questions:

- Who are your children?
- What are their lives like?

Regardless of where you teach—urban, suburban, or rural school—you will be faced with an increasingly diverse student population. Table 3.1 shows the dramatically changing demographics in schools in the United States, and Table 3.2 shows the ethnic and geographic distribution. Tables 3.1 and 3.2 have been developed using data from the U.S. Department of Education.

You will note that in two decades, the Hispanic and Asian population has almost doubled. This statistics has implications for the language of instruction and the need for cultural sensitivity. This changing demographics is also reflected in school enrollment in urban, suburban, and rural areas. It is not limited to urban schools. Hence all teachers have to develop strategies for dealing with an increasingly diverse student population.

Table 3.1 Percentage Distribution (rounded) of Public Elementary and Secondary School Enrollment, by Race/Ethnicity: Selected Years, 1986 to 2005

Year	White, non-Hispanic	Total minority[1]	Black, non-Hispanic	Hispanic	Asian/ Pacific Islander	American Indian/ Alaska Native
1986	70.4	29.6	16.1	9.9	2.8	0.9
1991	67.4	32.6	16.4	11.8	3.4	1.0
1996	64.2	35.8	16.9	14.0	3.8	1.1
2001	60.3	39.7	17.2	17.1	4.2	1.2
2005	57.1	42.9	17.2	19.8	4.6	1.2

[1]Total minority represents persons of all race/ethnicities other than white, non-Hispanic.

Note: Figures do not include students enrolled in Bureau of Indian Affairs (BIA) schools. Detail may not sum to totals because of rounding.

Source: U.S. Department of Education, Office for Civil Rights, *1986 state summaries of elementary and secondary school civil rights survey;* and National Center for Education Statistics, Common Core of Data (CCD), *Public elementary/secondary school universe survey, 1991–92 to 2005–06.*

Table 3.2 Enrollment in Public Elementary and Secondary Schools, by Race/Ethnicity and Locale: 2005–2006

Locale	Total	White, non-Hispanic	Black, non-Hispanic	Hispanic	Asian or Pacific Islander	American Indian/ Alaskan Native
All public schools	Percentage distribution					
	100.0	100.0	100.0	100.0	100.0	100.0
City	28.5	17.4	46.3	44.3	39.8	18.5
Suburban	36.1	37.2	31.2	35.8	45.9	15.3
Town	13.0	15.9	8.7	9.5	5.1	19.9
Rural	22.4	29.5	13.7	10.4	9.2	46.3

Note: Excludes enrollment for students whose race/ethnicity is unknown.

Source: U.S. Department of Education, National Center for Education Statistics (NCES), *The NCES Common Core of Data (CCD) survey, Public elementary/secondary school universe survey, 2005–06.*

What Are Your Class Demographics?

It might be useful to start the following activity as a private and confidential class profile. Refer to it as you develop your science lesson plans. The information collected here will enable you to respect and cultivate differences among your children.

Teacher Activity: What Are Your Class Demographics?

Class Profile	Traits
Gender	____ Number of students
	____ Girls
	____ Boys

(continued on next page)

Teacher Activity: What Are Your Class Demographics?
(continued)

Race   ___ American Indian

                                        ___ Asian

                                        ___ Pacific Islander

                                        ___ Filipino

                                        ___ Hispanic

                                        ___ African American

                                        ___ White

                                        ___ Multiple

                                        ___ no response

Religion   ___ Christian

                                        ___ Jewish

                                        ___ Muslim

                                        _____

Economic status   ___ Wealthy

                                        ___ Comfortable

                                        ___ Struggling

                                        ___ Poor

                                        ___ Homeless

Parent's occupation   ___ Parent 1

                                        ___ Parent 2

                                        ___ Caretaker/Guardian

Learning style (based on Gardner)   ___ Linguistic

                                        ___ Logical-mathematical

                                        ___ Spatial

                                        ___ Musical

                                        ___ Bodily-kinesthetic

                                        ___ Intrapersonal

                                        ___ Naturalist

(continued on next page)

Teacher Activity: What Are Your Class Demographics? (continued)

Languages	___ English
	___ Spanish
	___ Vietnamese
	_____
Special Needs	___ Fully able
	___ Disability
Technology at Home	___ Computer
	___ iPod
	_____
	_____
Types of Toys at Home	_____
	_____
	_____
	_____
Access to	___ Parks
	___ Gardens
	___ Backyards
Types of pets (if any)	_____
	_____

Reflect on your children as you complete this information. How can you use your knowledge of your class's profile to develop inclusive classroom activities?

_____

_____

_____

_____

The responses to the above questions will vary immensely, but here are some ways in which you can use this information to create an inclusive classroom. As an inclusive teacher who is aware of the diversity in your classroom, you must think about your teaching—what you teach, how you teach, and how you structure interactions among your children. All aspects of your classroom life must reflect your commitment to inclusiveness. As part of your curriculum, you should think critically about the kinds of display materials in your room. Do these materials model the belief that we all belong and can all contribute to science? Your books, posters, and other materials should include people of color and of various ethnic backgrounds and people with disabilities. A unit on the five senses should include a discussion on vision and hearing impairments. Consider physical abilities as you plan hands-on activities. Some of your children might not be able to participate in all activities; you might need to develop alternative experiences for them. Have your children work in mixed-gender groups and have each student occupy different roles. Let them all learn to handle materials and communicate what they are doing to the class.

How Can You Develop a Cultural Understanding of Your Children?

As we begin to develop a contextual framework for teaching K–2 science, let us first conduct an in-depth investigation and reflection on the children you teach and your understanding of their lived experiences.

Teacher Activity: Examining Your Classroom's Demographics

Examine your district, school, and class data and fill in the following table. You might find that you are unable to fill in all the columns and rows, but do as many as you can.

Demographics	State	District	School	Class
Parental Income Range				
Free Lunch				
English Learners				
Compensatory Education				
American Indian Asian Pacific Islander Filipino Hispanic African American White Other				
Males Females				

1. What differences do you notice between your state and the national data?

_____

_____

2. What differences do you notice between your class and your state data?

_____

_____

3. Has your district demographics experienced much change in the past 4–5 years?

_____

_____

4. Is your school experiencing any changing demographics?

_____

_____

Table 3.3 provides an example of demographics from an unnamed district and school on the West Coast.

Table 3.3 Example of Demographics of School and District

Demographics	District A	School 1
Free lunch	4,342	87
English language learners	2,459	44
Compensatory education	2,651	0
Instruction $/student	$3,649	No data available
Instruction—special education $/student	$1,037	No data available
American Indian	25	0
Asian	968	20
Pacific Islander	13	0
Filipino	585	10
Hispanic	6,010	116
African American	464	6
White	7,865	373
Multiple/no response	718	13

As you collect and closely examine this data and the data from your region, you will begin to see trends that will impact what and how you teach. If you are in an urban setting, for example, you might find yourself in a classroom with children who come from twenty to twenty-five different cultures, speak fifteen or more languages, practice twelve or more religions, come from one-parent homes or have two dads or two moms, are homeless, or are extremely wealthy. Those of you who are teaching in the urban setting are already aware of the changing demographics, and you need to be constantly learning about incoming cultures. You might be in a district that shows a beginning change in demographics, with the change not yet reaching your school or your classroom. Be alert. Demographics are changing. You need to begin thinking about how you will accommodate to the changing demographics. It is critical that you examine this data before you begin to plan for science. The data alerts you to the areas in which you must develop sensitivity and awareness, as well as the expectations that you can have of your children and their caregivers. It also helps you determine the types of activities that can be conducted.

Once you have some idea about the bigger picture, you next need to focus in on one diverse student and use this activity to begin to develop your understanding of children who are different. This type of activity is particularly useful if your children belong to a culture that is very different from your own culture. The place to begin is to collect some background information on what your children's lives are like.

Teacher Activity: Exploring Your Student's Lived Experiences

Visit the home of one student or talk to the student alone, or talk to parent(s)/guardian at a school meeting or by telephone, about

- expectations for student
- family-perceived views on education, science, future careers, jobs
- discipline
- homework rules
- frequency of family visits to museums, zoos, etc.

Pay special attention to available learning resources, cultural norms, gender roles, and expectations.

Reflect on what you have learned about this student, and develop a plan for integrating what you have discovered in developing teaching and learning strategies for that student.

After interviewing the parents or guardian of one student, you might want to talk to more parents during your parent-teacher meetings, or meet parents outside the school setting. Those who live in the community might already have this information. If you do not live or socialize in the community, you can use this activity as a means of beginning to develop your cultural understanding of your students.

Another good starting point in beginning to understand the new cultures that are moving into your community is the book *Common Bonds* (Byrnes and Kiger, 2005), which examines the growing diversity in schools in a constructive, empowering way.

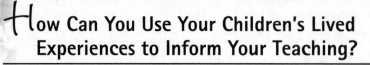

How Can You Use Your Children's Lived Experiences to Inform Your Teaching?

The data you have collected in the exercises in this section will inform your philosophical framework for teaching science. This information has implications for your student's access to science and technology materials, and field trips and for their knowledge of and interaction with scientists—all important issues you need to consider as you plan for teaching. You might already have been collecting such data for your teaching, but this information is of great importance as you plan for science teaching, since it will help you answer important questions such as:

- Can I expect my students' parents/guardians to help them with their science homework?

- Do I need to send letters home in English or another language?

- What do the parents do for a living? Can I reasonably expect them to provide some resources for me to teach science?

- What parents can I use as facilitators in my class when I expose my students to scientists and what they do?

- Do I have the child/children of a scientist(s) in my class?

- Do parents take their children to zoos, museums, and other nonformal institutions?

- Which parents can I invite to accompany my class on field trips?

- Are there any cultural/religious issues that I should be aware of?

Reflect on these questions and make some quick notes to yourself. What other questions could you add? You can refer back to these notes as you plan your teaching program later on.

What Are Your Expectations for Your Children?

It is acknowledged in the research community (Grayson and Martin, 2006) that

- People's perceptions about themselves and others shape their expectations for themselves and others in any interactive setting.

- The perceptions and expectations combine to determine how people act in any given situation.

- If a person is in a position of influence with another individual or group of individuals (e.g., teacher to student), the influential or more powerful person's perceptions, expectations, and behaviors have a direct impact on the achievement, success, and/or productivity of the individuals with whom he or she has the influence.

Teacher Activity: Teacher Expectations

Spend five to ten minutes quietly reflecting on your expectations for your children. Be as honest as you can be. These are your personal reflections. You do not have to share it with anyone.

1. What are your expectations for your students?

_____

_____

2. Where do you see them fitting into society fifteen to twenty years from now?

_____

_____

3. Will they be manual laborers, engineers, doctors, or teachers?

_____

_____

_____

4. Do you believe they can be scientists?

_____

5. Will they do well in school?

_____

6. Do you believe they can be scientifically literate? Literate?

_____

7. What do you think adults need to know about science to be productive members of society?

_____

_____

_____

Teacher Activity: Self-Reflection

What are the implications of these feelings for your teaching and your children's learning?

_____

_____

_____

_____

_____

_____

_____

_____

_____

_____

_____

_____

_____

_____

_____

How Can You Help Your K–2 Children Succeed in Science?

Teachers need to help both girls and boys develop the self-confidence and skills necessary to be successful. In today's classrooms, girls are rarely told they cannot do both mathematics and science. Textbooks show pictures of women and men in both career and nurturing roles. In preschools, little boys play in house-keeping center, and little girls play with trucks and blocks. Yet, although doors are opening, the data continue to show that young women have lower self-esteem, lower career aspirations, and lower rates of participation in math and science. Why? Part of the reason is that many women still face internal barriers to success. These are attitudes and fears that result from subtle differences in the ways in which girls and boys are socialized and interact with science. Even people who are trying to encourage girls may subconsciously be sending them negative messages. For example, well-intentioned math teachers may fear discouraging girls, so offer them less criticism than boys, thereby teaching them less. Or they may offer girls premature help, inadvertently suggesting to girls that they probably would not be able to solve the problem alone.

The following guidelines should help your children succeed in science. These interactions should begin in the K–2 classroom.

- Hold high expectations for all your children, especially for minority and female children. Research shows that positive expectations increase student achievement.

- Learn as much about minority and female children as other children in the classroom.

- Respond as fully to the comments of special needs, English language learners, minority, and female children as to other children.

- Encourage all children. Research shows that minority and female children receive less encouragement.

- Involve children who are not participating in classroom discussions. This may include a significant number of special needs, minority, and female children.

- Do not assume that assertive male children are more capable than female children.

- Make an effort to check classroom work of all children.

- Encourage all children to participate. Recognize that cultural backgrounds may discourage some children from active participation. In some ethnic groups, volunteering a response or comment is a sign of disrespect of authority.

- Monitor achievement of all children on a daily basis. This includes participation in classroom discussions and projects.

- Communicate belief in the potential of special needs, English language learners, minority, and female children in science. Many of these children underestimate their potential.

Teacher Activity: Final Self-Reflection

Finally, examine this question: How does knowing who your students are make you a more effective teacher?

_____

_____

_____

_____

_____

_____

_____

_____

_____

_____

Take-Away Thought

Children need to know that you care before they care about what you know.

The Inquiry Approach to Teaching and Learning Science

Focus Questions

- What is scientific inquiry?
- How can you develop inquiry skills?
- What are some inquiry-based teaching strategies?
- How can you use the process skills in inquiry teaching?
- How do you use process skills in your daily life?

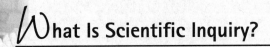

What Is Scientific Inquiry?

The vision of both the *Standards* and the *Benchmarks* is "science for all and scientific literacy for all." The way in which a child develops scientific literacy depends on experiences both inside and outside the classroom which will gradually help the child attain more complex modes of thinking. As science instruction in classrooms moves away from the lecture-based, teacher-dominated format, the roles of the teacher and the student change.

In an inquiry-based science learning environment, the teacher's role becomes one of a facilitator—a departure from the role of omniscient presence in the classroom. No longer is the teacher standing in front of the classroom delivering content; now, the teacher provides the type of environment which guides children to find the answers to the questions they have asked. The student subsequently becomes the master of her own learning as she progresses through her learning process making predictions, testing hypotheses, revising and ultimately answering questions, and deriving conclusions based on her findings. She is using science content knowledge and science processes together in science inquiry. When young children are engaged in inquiry, they

- ask questions
- plan investigations
- collect and interpret data
- share their findings

Scientific inquiry refers to the diverse ways in which scientists study the natural world and propose explanations based on the evidence derived from their work. Inquiry also refers to the activities of children in which they develop knowledge and understanding of scientific ideas, as well as an understanding of how scientists study the natural world. Inquiry is a multifaceted activity that involves

- making observations
- posing questions
- examining books and other sources of information to see what is already known
- planning investigations
- reviewing what is already known in light of experimental evidence
- using tools to gather, analyze, and interpret data

- proposing answers, explanations, and predictions
- communicating the results

Inquiry requires identification of assumptions, use of critical and logical thinking, and consideration of alternative explanations (NRC, 1996).

The *National Science Education Standards* call for more than "science as process," in which children learn such skills as observing, inferring, and experimenting. Inquiry is central to science learning. When engaging in inquiry, children describe objects and events, ask questions, construct explanations, test those explanations against current scientific knowledge, and communicate their ideas to others. They identify their assumptions, use critical and logical thinking, and consider alternative explanations. In this way, children actively develop their understanding of science by combining scientific knowledge with reasoning and thinking skills.

The importance of inquiry does not imply that all teachers should pursue a single approach to teaching science. Inquiry has many different facets, and teachers need to use many different strategies to develop the understandings and abilities described in the *Standards*. Furthermore, the *Standards* should not be seen as requiring a specific curriculum. A curriculum is the way content is organized and presented in the classroom. The content embodied in the *Standards* can be organized and presented with many different emphases and perspectives in many different curricula.

How Can You Develop Inquiry Skills?

Science is, in fact, a combination of both content and process—learning about the body of knowledge that exists and actively exploring answers to questions you generate about the body of knowledge. We want our K–2 children to learn science by "doing" science, to learn science by generating their own questions, and to seek answers to their own questions. It is important for children to have endless "Why" "How" "What" questions as they interact with their classroom environment and the environment they encounter outside of the classroom.

To teach science well means presenting lessons using strategies that encourage children to better understand the natural world and that actively involve them in discovery that helps them understand what scientists do and find answers to their questions. You want your children to emerge as scientists with endless questions. One way of doing this is to set up a question board in your classroom.

Teacher Activity: The Why Board

Children will write their questions on the board as they are generated. Once or twice per week, set aside a few minutes for "Who has found an answer?" time. Let two or three children tell the class what they now know and what else they want to find out.

Teaching science using inquiry involves having questions generated by children direct their learning experiences. This activity allows your children the time to find answers to the questions they generated.

For example, Nicolas, a kindergartener, had a question about dinosaurs. "How big are dinosaurs?" This question led to a trip to the science museum with his parents. For his "Who has found an answer?" time he showed this picture.

His next question was "Are dinosaurs bigger than all other animals?" This led to yet another trip and a comparison of the size of dinosaurs and other animals at the science museum. In the ensuing class discussion, children compared the sizes of dinosaurs, elephants, and other large animals and concluded that some dinosaurs are bigger than elephants, while others were smaller. Later questions were

- How can I measure a dinosaur?
- Where can I find dinosaurs?

As your children find answers, let them talk about, draw, or write their responses to share with the rest of the class. You need to keep nurturing this question-asking nature in your emerging scientists, and you need to frame your curriculum around these questions.

Do not supply your children with answers. The emphasis should be on them being scientists and finding answers by investigation, by using the science process skills. One of the most astonishing discoveries a nonscientist can make about science is that there are far more questions than there are answers. It is the asking of questions that makes science so dynamic, and it is the constant searching for the most probable answers that occupies a great deal of scientists' time and efforts. Young children are at the beginning of this question-asking journey. They are emerging scientists! Children are natural investigators. They are always ready to ask questions. Inquiry science comes naturally to them. As teachers, your role is to foster the growth of inquiry and to deeply embed in your K–2 children the desire to ask questions and to find answers to these questions.

Here are examples of questions that might appear on your Why Board:

- Why does the blue triangle not fit in the square hole?
- Why does the butterfly keep coming back to this flower?
- Why does the snowflake disappear when it hits the ground?
- What is a snowflake made out of?
- How does this watch work?
- Where does the sun go when it goes to bed?
- Why do some things float while others sink?
- Why do some objects stick to a magnet while others do not?

These questions represent the beginning of inquiry for your children. Your role is to provide them with the resources to help them find the answers to their questions.

What Are Some Inquiry–Based Teaching Strategies?

Barab and Luehmann (2002), in their research on science teaching, suggest that there is a call for a "new approach" to science education. Central to this call is a shift from a focus on supporting acquisition of formal science content to promoting a culture of scientific literacy by engaging children in the language and ways of scientific inquiry. There should be a shift in the way that science is taught. This shift is from a more traditional lecture-driven science curriculum to a more active, inquiry-based curriculum. The authors propose that the driving force behind the movement to an inquiry curriculum can be attributed to a view of children as global citizens rather than as vessels to be filled with facts. Subsequently, science education should attempt to provide children with a better understanding of the world around them while recognizing that not all of them will be future scientists

In order to approach science in a novel way, moving away from rote memorization of facts for later regurgitation, the literature suggests that it is important to engage children in scientific inquiry. This scientific inquiry should be in the context of authentic and sustained scientific investigations, allowing children to not only learn the content of science but also to master the inquiry/doing process of science as well.

By the time children begin school, they will have lived scientifically for at least a few years. They have been curious, have identified problems, have asked questions, and have sought answers. School science, when it is offered, adds a new dimension, with children now being guided in their quest for answers through the provision of carefully selected learning activities, materials, and teaching strategies. In the K–2 classroom, where children are continuously generating their own questions, inquiry, guided discovery, and problem-based learning strategies are most applicable.

Guided Discovery

Children begin with questions and materials that will help them find answers to the questions. Your class can be divided up into small groups and given the time to observe, explore, and discover the answers to the questions. As your children explore, you serve as the facilitator or guide to this discovery. As facilitator, you are responsible for

- supplying the initial question/s to initiate exploration
- providing relevant materials/resources

- listening to each group as they explore
- keeping them on track with their exploration
- providing materials which will move the exploration forward

As children explore, you must always keep in mind that *they have to come up with their answers; you are not there to supply the answers.* Always redirect questions to them by using responses such as What do you think? or Can you try out your partner's idea? You allow children the time to explore, to "mess about" with the materials, and in the process to find answers to their interesting questions. As you move around the class, you should give only minimal assistance to ensure that children are not unduly frustrated and quit. You must not tell children what you want them to learn or give answers. You want them to discover the answers on their own, with minimal guidance from you. When using this method, the question could be generated by the children, the text, the lesson plan, or you. You can help children seek text-based answers if they cannot find answers through their own material exploration.

In summary, during guided discovery you will

- engage children in activities
- encourage them to explore concrete materials and reflect upon their findings
- engage children in conversations, listen to their ideas, and provide guidance to help them build and test their own explanations of what is happening (Koch, 1999, p. 12)

Problem-Based Learning

Children are presented with a challenge (such as a question to be answered, an observation or data set to be interpreted, or a hypothesis to be tested) and will accomplish the desired learning in the process of responding to that challenge. As with all inductive methods, the information needed to address the challenge would not have been previously covered explicitly in class or readings. Children usually working in teams are confronted with an open-ended, real-world problem to solve and take the lead in defining the problem precisely and in figuring out what they know, what they need to determine, and how to proceed in determining it. They formulate and evaluate alternative solutions, select the best one and make a case for it, and evaluate the lesson learned. When they identify the need for instruction on new material, the instructor either provides it or guides the children to obtain the required information themselves. In problem-based learning, children have not previously received formal instruction in the necessary background material, and the solution process is more important than the final product.

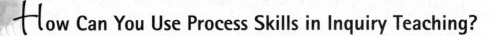

How Can You Use Process Skills in Inquiry Teaching?

To be good inquiry learners, we must develop and use process skills, since these are the building blocks of inquiry.

Every day is filled with opportunities to learn science. We can begin with introducing our young children to the natural world by encouraging them to observe what goes on around them. You can guide them to

- see how long it takes for a dandelion or a rose to burst into full bloom

- watch the moon as it appears to change shape over the course of a month and record the changes

- watch a caterpillar change into a butterfly

- bake a cake

- guess why one of your plants is drooping

The processes of science are basic components of thinking and are useful in problem solving and critical thinking, not only in science but also in day-to-day life situations. As young children enter school, it is critical to emphasize individual processes to help them become proficient in using the processes. They are then introduced to activities in which the use of processes is combined with domain-specific knowledge, as determined by the *Benchmarks*. As you research the process skills, you will find a variation from state to state or program to program.

These skills represent the range of activities in which scientists engage and which children need to become fully scientifically literate and capable critical thinkers.

A comprehensive and representative list of process skills is included in *Teaching Budding Scientists* (Table 4.1). In this book, we focus on six key process skills that are critical for K–2 children: observing, classifying, measuring, communicating, predicting, and inferring. In grades 3–5, children build on those skills and acquire others, and by grades 6–8, they must be competent in the use of all these skills. A list of these process skills is included in Table 4.1.

Teacher Activity: Process Skills

Go to your state Website and print out the process skills that are listed. Check column 3 of Table 4.1 if the skills are used in your state.

Table 4.1 Process Skills

Process Skill	Definition	Check if listed for your state
Observing	becoming aware of an object or event by using any of the senses to identify properties	
Measuring	making quantitative observations by comparing to a conventional or nonconventional standard	
Classifying	sorting objects, events, or information representing objects or events in classes, according to some method or system	
Communicating	giving oral or written explanations or graphic representations of observations	
Inferring	drawing a conclusion based on prior experiences	
Predicting	making a forecast of future events or conditions expected to exist	

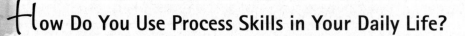

How Do You Use Process Skills in Your Daily Life?

In your day-to-day activities, you, too, use these skills. There are many daily instances in which you must act like a scientist.

Teacher Activity: A Damaged Computer

Your computer has been damaged in a flood at your school. How do you solve this problem? What do you do? Should you dump it? Can it be saved? List the steps you take and the questions you ask. List the process skills you engage in as you make a decision.

_____

_____

_____

_____

_____

_____

_____

_____

_____

_____

_____

_____

_____

_____

_____

_____

_____

_____

Before you purchase an appliance (such as a washing machine), you spend time investigating the pros and cons of one brand versus another. You are curious about energy consumption, level of noise, load capacity, control panel, etc. You analyze the product in terms of your needs. You go on the Internet and check consumer reports. You ask friends who have the brands you are interested in, compare prices, check for sales, and finally make an objective decision based on your tentative conclusions. You then buy the product that best meets your needs. In the investigation, you have used many of the processes that scientists use as they engage in science. This is yet another reason to develop students' scientific skills.

Take-Away Thought

Everyone uses process skills in their daily decision making.

5

Exploring Process Skills

Focus Questions

- How can you develop observation skills?
- How can you develop measuring skills?
- How can you develop communication skills?
- How can you develop classification skills?
- How can you develop predicting skills?
- How can you develop inference-making skills?
- How well do you know the process skills?

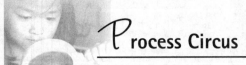

Process Circus

It is critical that, as a K–2 teacher, you experience the processes so that you can better incorporate them in your inquiry teaching.

The following activity could best be used by a staff developer to introduce teachers to the science process skills.

Teacher Activity: Process Circus

Purpose: To clarify the meaning of each process skill in practical action terms, and to arrive at a group understanding of the process skills.

Procedure:
- Brief introduction
- Practical work on circus
- Small group discussions to combine results and reflect upon the meaning of each process skill
- Whole group plenary discussion

Preparation: You should create 10–14 brief practical items, each of which has a specific process skill as its main focus. Here are examples of six items with required equipment *in italics*:

1. Draw and label what you think a candle looks like when it is lit. Light the candle and draw it again. What is different from what you first drew? *Candle and matches.*

2. Measure the amount of water that drips from the tap in one minute. Work out how much water will drip away in one day. *10 or 25 ml measuring cylinder, stop-clock, sink with tap dripping at a steady pace.*

3. If you have three different types of soil, how would you tell which holds the most water?

4. Put ice in the can. Look at the outside of the can. Write down as many possible explanations of what you see as you can. *Clean empty shiny can without lid, ice cubes.*

5. Every twig tells the story of its own life. Closely examine your twig and tell the story of its life. *Twig with buds and scars, but no leaves or flowers, hand lens.*

6. Divide the leaves into as many groups as you can. *10–12 varying colored and shaped fall leaves.*

Write each item on a card and lay them out around the room in any order. Each item should have the required equipment.

Introduction: Participants are asked to work in pairs to carry out the task on each card using only the equipment given. They use the following grid for recording their decisions about the process skills they use in carrying out each task.

(continued on next page)

Teacher Activity: Process Circus (continued)

Process skills/Circus item	1	2	3	4	5	6
Observing						
Measuring						
Communicating						
Classifying						
Predicting						
Inferring						

Each group is to indicate by checking off in the grid for each item the process skills which they judge that they used. There may be more than one process skill and it may be that some are felt to be predominant in an item. They can use their own way of indicating this weighting.

Practical work: Participants go around the "circus" carrying out the activities. They must do what is on the card and not just read and respond without carrying out the task themselves. This ensures that they experience the process and can reflect on what they actually did, not just the verbal description. After each activity they must also fill in the above grid about the process skills used.

Small group discussion: Participants are now formed into groups of 6-8 to discuss each item of the circus and to try to arrive at a group consensus on the process skills used. Where there are differences, they must justify their views. In doing so, differing views about the meaning of the process skills are revealed and the discussion helps individual members refine and revise their own ideas.

Plenary discussion: One group is chosen to present its results item by item. Other groups will report on differences between what is presented and their own views. These differences have to be reconciled by appeal to evidence of the circus items, justification from the group or by reference to the indicators found at the end of each process section in the chapter. At all times the purpose of the exercise should be kept in mind, i.e. the clarification and greater shared understanding of the process skills. At the end of this discussion participants should arrive at definitions which they have helped to generate for each process skill and should all have a better understanding of each process skill. Participants will note that often, it is not possible to tease out a single process from an activity, since the processes tend to be closely interwoven (e.g., you cannot communicate without first observing or classify without first observing). It is virtually impossible to present each process as a discrete, isolated, totally unique action. Often, you will be using several skills in order to better understand one particular skill. You will soon see that the overlap and interplay among the processes is not only inevitable but also essential in scientific inquiry.

The following activities are designed to involve teachers in developing an understanding of the process skills followed by reflection, analysis and development of process based activities for their own classroom.

How Can You Develop Observation Skills?

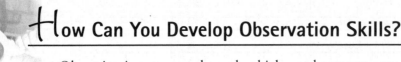

Observing is a process through which you become aware of objects and events. Observation involves the use of any one of the senses alone (touch, taste, smell, sight, and hearing) or the senses in combination. Observing is a skill that can always be improved. No one can ever say that they have mastered the skill of observing. Generally, the more opportunities you have for observing, the more you will improve your use of this skill. The following activity can strengthen both your skill of observing and your awareness of your environment.

Teacher Activity: A Ten-Minute Observation Walk

Take a ten-minute walk around your school.

1. What do you see? (trees, cracks in the school wall, etc.)

_____

2. What do you hear? (water dripping, loud music, birds, crickets, etc.)

_____

3. What do you smell? (car exhaust, leaves, etc.)

_____

4. Is there anything in the environment that you can taste? (clover, water, etc.)

_____

5. What can you touch? (rough surfaced wall, etc.)

_____

Classroom Activity: Writing Observation Activities

Safety note: Because of health concerns, you must not allow young children to taste without permission from parents. Before involving them in an activity involving taste you should send a letter home to parents and get their written consent.

Encourage your children to observe nature using all of their senses. Based on what you have just done, write two simple observing activities for use with your class.

1. First observation activity

   _____

   _____

2. Second observation activity

   _____

   _____

Process Indicator

Children are observing when they can

- identify properties of objects (such as color, size, and shape) by using any or all of the senses and can answer this type of question: What do you notice about these objects?

- state noticeable changes in objects or event and can answer this type of question: What changes do you notice?

- state noticeable similarities and differences in objects or events and can answer this type of question: How are they alike? Different?

How Can You Develop Measuring Skills?

By measuring, we are able to increase the precision of our observations and provide a means of recording our observations. We must decide what measurements should be taken and what instruments should be used. Should we use a measuring cylinder, a ruler, or a balance? What units should we use?

Teacher Activity: Measurement

The following activities will involve you in the process of measuring. You will make linear measurements, liquid measurements, and mass/weight measurements.

1. Linear measurement

   Select a nonstandard measuring device, identify it by some means, and measure the same object or distance in the room using the selected device. Body parts such as hands, feet, or arms make good nonstandard measuring devices.

   Record your data.

   - Identify your measuring device.

   - Identify what was measured.

   - Identify the distance measured.

   - Is the recorded measurement consistent with the type of measuring device used? For example, if you selected a paper clip as the measuring device, the object or distance measured should be recorded as so many paper clips in length.

   - If you are working with a partner, did you use the same device for measuring? For example, if you both chose to use a hand as the measuring device, then the same hand must be used for all measurements. Hands come in different sizes, as do other devices that might be used in measuring distances. It is very important that a standard be established so that measurement can be related.

2. Liquid measurement

   Select two containers: one should be much larger than the other. Identify each by some means and use the smaller container to determine the amount of liquid that the larger container holds.

   Record your data.

   - Identify your measuring device.

   - Identify what was measured.

(continued on next page)

Teacher Activity: Measurement (continued)

- Identify the amount measured.

- Is the recorded measurement consistent with the type of measuring device used? For example, if you identified the measuring device as "a small cup," then the amount recorded should be in so many small cups.

- Did you establish a way to handle the problem of describing the amount measured when the measuring device was only partially filled? If not, do so now.

3. Mass/weight measurements

Select an object and measure its mass/weight using an equal-arm balance. Place the object to be measured on one side of the balance and measure its mass/weight by placing paper clips on the other side until it balances.

Record your data.

- Identify the object to be measured.

- What was the mass/weight of the object?

- Is the mass/weight of the object recorded so that it is clear that paper clips were the standard?

- What other things could you use as a standard for measuring mass/weight?

When you have completed the three parts of this activity, answer the following:

- How were you involved in the process of measuring?

  _____

  _____

  _____

- Can you explain this process?

  _____

  _____

  _____

- How important is it to identify a standard when making measurements?

  _____

  _____

  _____

Classroom Activity: Write Measuring Activities

Now that you have had some experience with measuring, how can you transfer these ideas to your classroom? Write three measuring activities that you can use.

1. Activity 1

_____

_____

2. Activity 2

_____

_____

3. Activity 3

_____

_____

Process Indicator

Children are measuring when they can

- arrange objects in sequence by length (shortest to longest), weight (lightest to heaviest), volume (least to greatest), chronologically (beginning to end), numerically (in ordinal order)

- use standard tools—such as the meter stick, yardstick, ruler, clock, balance, and protractor—to find quantity

How Can You Develop Communication Skills?

Communication is conveying information by means of oral or written descriptions, pictures, graphs, maps, or demonstrations. Communicating in science refers to the skill of describing simple phenomena. A written or oral description of physical objects and systems and of the changes in them is one of the most common ways of communicating in science. Communicating takes many forms—identifying, matching, sorting, naming, comparing, contrasting, grouping, distinguishing likenesses and differences, relating observations, and using words accurately Drawings, data charts, graphs, and journals are all used in recording and communicating descriptions of science experiences and results of experimentation.

Teacher Activity: Communicating with a Friend

This activity will involve you in the process of communicating. You need to work with a partner to complete this communicating activity. Take a walk with a friend. As you walk, begin to describe an object that you have selected. You must describe the object so clearly and accurately that your partner must be able to identify it on the first try.

Communicating serves two purposes:

- to ensure that knowledge of concepts and relationships is accurately recorded
- to share findings with others

Classroom Activity: Communicating

Now that you have had some experience with communicating, how can you transfer these ideas to your classroom? Write two communicating activities for use with your class.

1. Activity 1

_____

2. Activity 2

_____

Process Indicator

Children are communicating when they

- describe objects or events and can answer this type of question: How can you describe this _____ so someone else knows what you mean?

- make charts and graphs and can answer this type of question: How can you make a chart or graph to show your findings?

- record data as needed and can answer this type of question: How can we keep track of our observations?

- construct exhibits and models and can answer this type of question: How can we show someone how this works?

- draw diagrams, pictures, and maps and can answer these types of questions: What can we draw to explain what happens? What map can you draw so someone else can find the place?

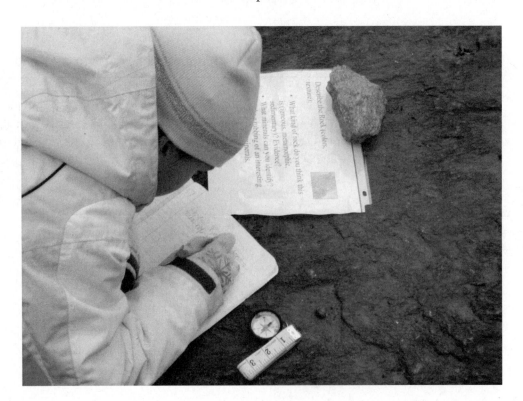

How Can You Develop Classification Skills?

As children engage in classifying, they are identifying, matching, sorting, naming, comparing, contrasting, grouping, and distinguishing likenesses and differences.

One of the ways in which knowledge obtained from scientific inquiry can be organized is through classification. For example, plants and animals are two of the five major kingdoms into which living things in the world can be grouped. Within each there are subclasses, and within these, there are more subclasses. This system provides a way to organize a vast amount of information. However K–2 children are at the beginning stages of classification. They may be able to learn that something is an animal, that it is a mammal, and further, that it is a dog, but the information remains specific and not integrated in the child's mind. At this stage they are not yet able to fathom the five kingdoms.

Teacher Activity: Classifying Animals

Classify the animals in the picture based on criteria you have selected.

1. Identify and label each group according to the property you used to separate the groups.

   a. Organize the pictures into two groups. Record the property used to make the separation.

   b. Find another way to separate the pictures into two groups. Label the two new groups.

   c. Take about three minutes and see how many different ways you can divide the pictures into two groups. Label each group.

2. Now that you have had some practice in grouping, or classifying, objects into two sets, try to separate the pictures into three groups. Make as many sets of these as you can and label them.

3. Check over your list to see that all the pictures fit into one of the groups in each set. But make sure that no one picture could fit into both groups of one set.

$\mathcal{T}$eacher $\mathcal{A}$ctivity: Questions to Develop Classifying Skills

If you were trying to help children develop the skill of classifying, what questions might you ask to encourage them to investigate the various properties that could be used in grouping the objects?

List some questions:

_____

_____

_____

_____

_____

_____

Process Indicator

Children are classifying when they

- group objects or events by their properties or functions and can answer questions such as In what ways could we group these objects?

- arrange objects or events in order by some properties or value and can answer questions such as How could we put these objects in order?

Classification Activities

The activities that follow below are part of a series of activities on classification from the program at the New York Hall of Science, taught by Preeti Gupta, vice president of education, and Frank Signorelli, director of science programs. This is what they say about their experience with the lesson.

> When we model this lesson in professional development, we allow teachers to experience the process of science as K–2 learners. Student objectives addressed in this lesson allow the learner to practice or experience one aspect of the process of science—the sorting and classification of insects.
>
> In the lesson modeling, not only do teachers become students, they also receive a model of what science teaching on a given topic can look like. They can see how each activity reinforces the big idea as well as how each activity builds on the previous one. They can see where to embed multiple learning styles, how to assess prior knowledge, and how to assess content and understanding at the end of the unit.
>
> This activity demonstrates a structure for science lessons that the New York Hall of Science has found to be the most effective. In this activity, there are two types of motivational activities. The first is an inquiry starter, where children get a "bag of stuff" and then sort it using teacher-determined criteria.

This addresses the tactile learners. The second activity is a read-aloud, which engages the verbal and auditory learners. Inquiry starters and motivational read-aloud's are great assessment tools for prior knowledge.

The next activity, where children get a bag of bugs to sort, is a focused investigation. Children use the same teacher criteria to sort the bugs at first. Then they are invited to create their own criteria for classification. Allowing children to develop their own criteria provides an opportunity for them to develop higher-order thinking skills for classification.

The final activity, the worksheet, serves as a nonthreatening assessment tool, because the teacher can figure out the extent to which children have learned the process of sorting and classifying. When concluding the activities, the teacher can start a conversation with children about other things that can be sorted and classified, such as plants, rocks, stars, etc.

CLASSY CLASSIFICATION

Grade: First

Time frame: Approximately 45 minutes

Purpose: Through various hands-on activities, the children will learn the differences between insects and spiders and how they are classified.

Objectives: At the end of the lesson the children will be able to
- sort by color, shape, and size
- list characteristics that make an insect an insect

Overview

Introduction: What are entomologists?

Activity 1: Sort objects by color, shape, and size

Activity 2: Read *Bugs Are Insects* by Anne Rockwell

Activity 3: Classify insects

Activity 4: Worksheet

Conclusion

Materials:

Per pair of children: baggie with random objects, baggie of bugs

Per student: crayons, worksheets

Book: *Bugs Are Insects*

Introduction and Inquiry Starter

Everyone here is a scientist. Today, you are going to be special scientists called entomologists. Have the children repeat the word and then ask if anyone has any ideas on who they are and what they do. *They study something very small. They are scientists that study insects. Can you name any insects?* It's OK if they name things that are not insects; hopefully some of the children will name spiders, centipedes, or other noninsects, then later they can go back to the list and correct it with the new information they've learned.

Activity 1. Sort objects by color, shape, and size

Entomologists classify insects by the shape of their mouth; if they have wings, the shape of their legs. Do you know what it means to classify? To classify means to sort or group by certain criteria.

Give each pair of children a baggie of random objects and have them sort this baggie using the criteria of their choice.

Children will work in pairs and practice sorting by

- color
- shape
- size (small vs. big paper clips, squares, and circles)

Allow the children two to three minutes to sort by each criteria. Then ask them to name some of the colors and some of the shapes they sorted by.

Note: Some of the objects are small, so tell the children to be careful with them and try not to lose them or put them in their mouth. Have the children look on the floor afterward just to make sure none have dropped.

Activity 2. Read *Bugs Are Insects* (pp 1–17, 28–31)

After reading the book, review by asking the children some questions:

- *How many legs do insects have?* (six)
- *How many body parts do insects have?* (three—head, thorax, abdomen)
- *Are spiders insects?* (No.)
- *Why? How many legs do spiders have?* (eight)
- *How many body parts do spiders have?* (two—cephalothorax and abdomen)
- *Insects have exoskeletons while we have internal skeletons. But not everything that has an exoskeleton is an insect.*

Activity 3. Classify Insects

Hand out the baggie of insects to each learning pair of children. Tell the children that all of the insects are plastic so there's nothing to be alarmed about. *Using what we learned earlier, we will work in pairs to classify these insects by the following criteria:*

- color
- shape (butterflies, spiders, grasshoppers, etc.)
- wings or no wings
- six legs or more than six legs

With older children (second-graders), you can have them list different ways we can classify these insects. Then classify by the ways they suggest. Have them formulate their own criteria for sorting.

Note: Some of the plastic insects have wings that are closed and remind the children that antennae are not legs. *Be careful with the butterflies, they have very delicate wings.*

Activity 4. Worksheet

This is the last page of this lesson plan; answers are on the following page.

- Pass out crayons to the tables.
- The children will circle or color in only the insects.
- You will then assess what they've learned.
- *How do you know it's an insect? Count its legs and body parts.*

There are five insects on the worksheet. (Insect K has one pair of legs that are not visible in the drawing.)

Figure 5.1 Worksheet for Classifying Insects

Name _____   Date _____

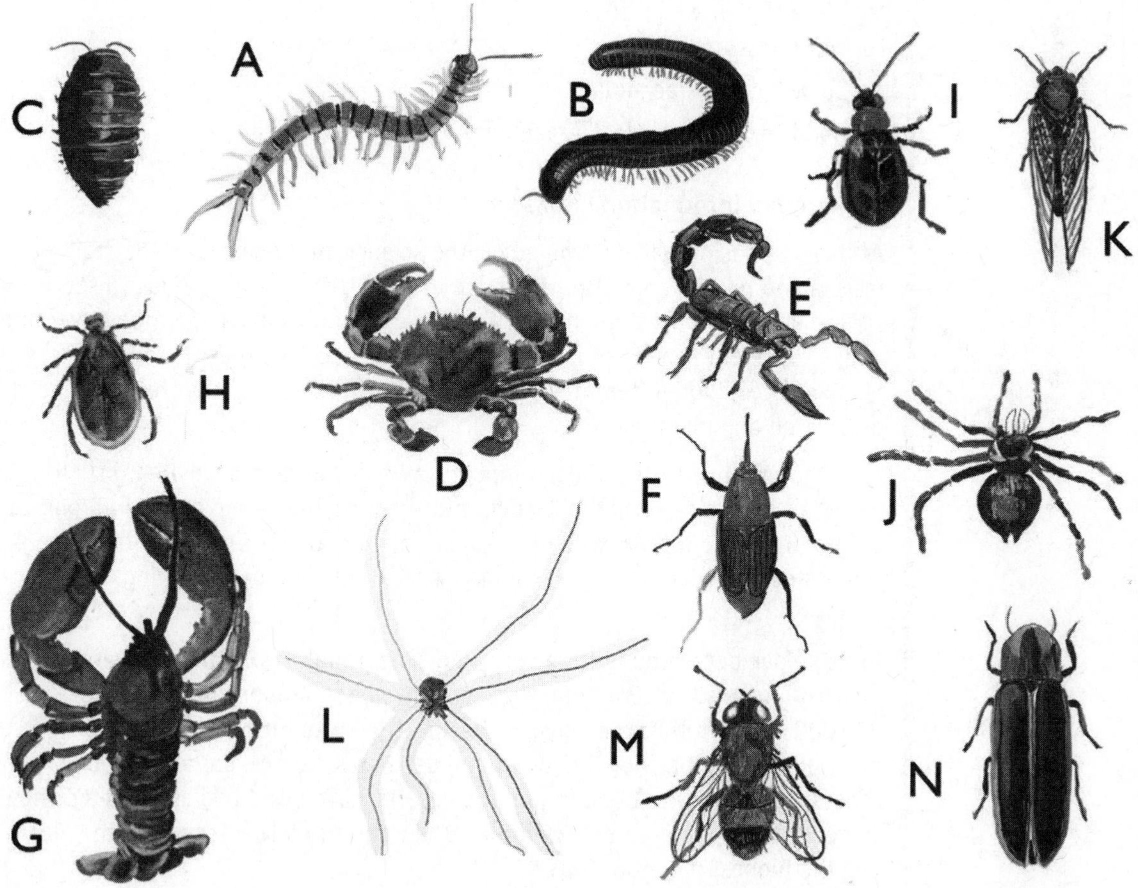

There are 5 insects on the page. Circle or color in the ones you think are insects.

Answers for Worksheet

Here's how the class Insecta in Figure 5.1 can be recognized as insects:

F.   has six legs and wings (wings may not be obvious in the drawing)

I.   wingless, but has three body regions and three pairs of legs

K.   three body regions and obviously winged (one pair of legs not visible in the drawing)

M.   three body regions, obvious wings, and three pairs of legs

N.   three pairs of legs

All the other arthropods shown have too many legs to be insects. They are

A.   Centipede (class Chilopoda)

B.   Millipede (class Diplopoda)

C.   Sowbug (class Crustacca)

D.   Crab (class Crustacea)

E.   Scorpion (class Arachnida)

G.   Crayfish (class Crustacea)

H.   Tick (class Arachnida)

J.   Spider (class Arachnida)

L.   Daddy-Long Legs (class Arachnida)

Background Information on Insects

At its most basic level, entomology is the science that deals with the study of insects and related animals. Insects are members of the animal class Insecta, by far the largest group of animals in the world. While we have identified over one million different species of insects, some experts believe that there may be as many as 30 million different species of insects in the world that have not been discovered and identified yet.

Even though they exist in huge numbers, all adult insects have a hard shell called an exoskeleton that is divided into three sections—the head, with one pair of antennae; the thorax, with six legs; and the abdomen, which contains the "guts" and reproductive organs. Some insects have two pairs of wings on their thorax.

Insects have been around for a very long time, roughly 350 million years, while modern humans (modern homo sapiens) have been around for only about 200,000 years. In that time, insects have settled into nearly every environment on the planet. They are all around us—in our homes, gardens, schools, and offices. They also are found in jungles, deserts, caves, and bodies of water. They can even be found in unexpected places like the frigid North and South Poles and the highest mountaintops.

The study of insects helps us understand the physiology and biology of other animals. The actions of insects help us comprehend animal behavior. We can also learn about the environment by studying insects. For example, the quantity and quality of insect life in and around a pond can indicate the presence or absence of pollution.

Figure 5.2 Parts of Insects

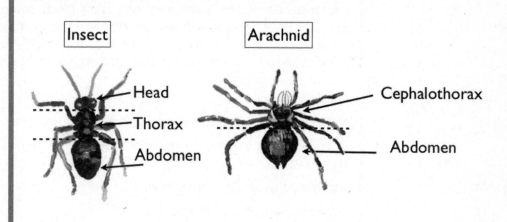

Considering that there are a lot of insects found nearly everywhere on the planet, it is no wonder some people devote their lives and careers to studying insects and their relationships to the environment, humans, and other organisms. Every year, these scientists, called entomologists, make great contributions to many fields of science.

Parts of Insects

The Head

The main visible parts on the head are the large compound eyes, the antenna (feelers), and the mouthparts. On the grasshopper, the antennae are long and threadlike. Grasshoppers have chewing-type mouthparts, but other insects may have sucking, rasping, or undeveloped mouthparts.

The Thorax

The thorax is the middle region of the body, and it bears the legs and wings; wings are present. The front wing is long, narrow, and somewhat leathery on the grasshopper. The hind wing is membranous and folds like a fan under the front wing when the grasshopper is not flying.

Almost all insects have a pronotum covering the top of the first segment of the thorax, but it is usually not as big as on a grasshopper. On the grasshopper, it looks like a saddle behind the head. Near the base of the middle leg, there is a small breathing hole called the thoracic spiracle. Insects breathe through spiracles and not through their mouths.

The legs of different insects are adapted to do different things. The legs of some insects are adapted for swimming, burrowing, jumping, or grasping. From looking at the form of the grasshopper's hind leg, how do you suppose they are used?

The Abdomen

The abdomen does not have many outstanding features on most insects. It just looks like a series of similar looking segments. On some grasshoppers, there is a large round disc on the first segment next to the thorax. It is called a tympanum and is the grasshopper's ear. If you look closely at the other abdominal segments, you can find a pinhole on the side of each segment. They are abdominal spiracles and are also used for breathing just like the spiracle on the thorax.

Conclusion

You know lots of facts about insects! Let's review the things we have learned.

Is there anything on our list of insects that we should cross off and now know that they aren't insects?

How many legs do insects have? (six)

How many body parts do they have? (three)

Now you are all entomologists.

(For additional information see http://www.smm.org/sln/tf/s/segment/segment.html and http://www.uky.edu/Agriculture/Entomology/ythfacts/4h/unit1/insects.gif.)

How Can You Develop Predicting Skills?

Predicting is the ability to state a future occurrence based on a pattern formed from previous observations. A prediction can only be made after a series of observations and measurements have been made and their relationships determined. On the basis of the analysis of collected data, you can predict or forecast what will happen next. In order to make a reasonable prediction, you must be clear about the difference between a guess and a prediction. A guess is a statement based on no data or very little data. A prediction is a statement based on a lot of data. You should write down your data and then look for a pattern. You may need to prepare a graph and extend the graph, following the pattern it seems to follow.

By developing skills of thinking systematically and logically about what might happen next, you can begin to think about planning ahead. Making a prediction is very different from just guessing; predictions should be based on selected data. Two types of predictions are possible using graphically presented data: (1) interpolation, within the data, and (2) extrapolation, beyond the data. In both types of predictions, data are gathered and recorded in graph form. A pattern should emerge and the prediction is then made. The following activity is designed to help you engage in the process of predicting.

Teacher Activity: Predicting Dissolving Time

If two sugar cubes take a certain time to dissolve in water at room temperature, and dissolve faster and faster as you increase the temperature from 10°C to 20°C to 40°C, you may form a pattern with respect to the time the cubes take to dissolve as the temperature increases. So, you may be able to predict how long sugar cubes will take to dissolve at a temperature of 60°C. You may draw a graph to help in your prediction.

Plan two activities for your class involving the use of predicting.

1. Activity 1

_____

_____

_____

_____

2. Activity 2

_____

_____

_____

_____

Children are predicting when they

- think systematically and logically about what might happen next
- begin to think about planning ahead

How Can You Develop Inference-Making Skills?

It is important that you learn to distinguish between observations and inferences. An observation is made through one or more of the senses. An inference is an explanation of an observation or a number of observations. The inference you make may be reasonable, but it may or may not be correct. An inference could be described as an educated guess. It is an interpretation or an explanation based on observations. It is a speculation from immediate observation.

Teacher Activity: Making Inferences

Example: You were sleeping for the last hour. You get up and you go outside. The ground is wet, the car is wet. You can see and feel that the ground and the car are wet, so these are observations. You did not see rain falling, so if you say that rain fell, you are making an inference. Your inference may or may not be correct. Someone could have sprayed the ground and the car with a garden hose. However, your inference is a reasonable one.

List examples of two inferences:

1. _____

   _____

   _____

   _____

2. _____

   _____

   _____

   _____

Children are inferring when they

- understand that their explanations of an observation may be reasonable but may or may not be correct

One of the greatest benefits of being able to distinguish between an observation and an inference is a decrease in the tendency to jump to conclusions. Observations help us become more aware of our world, and adequate use of inferences makes us more curious as well as more cautious in jumping to conclusions. Inferences should always be tentative, limited, subjective, and informed by previous experiences.

How Well Do You Know the Process Skills?

You can ask questions to start children thinking about any of the process skills, as in the following activity.

Classroom Activity: Matching Skills

Below is a list of process skills and questions. Each question goes with one of the skills. Match each question with the proper skill involved.

Process skills

A. observing

B. classifying

C. measuring

D. communicating

E. predicting

Question clusters

- What do you think will happen?
- What did you find out? What story do the small footprints tell?
- How could you put these objects together? In what groups do they belong?
- How could these things be put into some order?
- What do you notice?
- How are these objects alike? Different?
- How does this compare to how it was before?
- How heavy (light, fast, slow, tall, etc.) is it?
- What could you use instead of a meter stick?
- How can you estimate how many peas are in a jar?
- How can you show your findings on a chart?
- How can you keep a record of your plant work?

Answers: E, D, B, B, A, A, A, C, C, C, D, D

Take-Away Thought

Your students emerge as scientists when they use their senses to observe, measure, classify, communicate, predict, infer, experiment.

Establishing Your Science Program

6

Focus Questions

- What are the Big Ideas in science?

- What concepts should you include in your curriculum?

- How do you build an effective science learning classroom environment?

- How can you set up your classroom for science?

Remember, you are not alone in teaching science. There are numerous resources all around you. Many of them you have not thought of, many of them you do not know exist, and many you pass by on a daily basis and do not think of as a science teaching resource. Do you know that you can take your class on a field trip in your school? Let us begin to prepare for teaching science to young children. We will first consider what content we need to know to begin the journey. Then we will examine the numerous resources that you can use to help you on your journey. In order to assist you in your preparation, you will find in the appendixes:

- the requirements of the *National Science Education Standards,* the *Benchmarks for Science Literacy*, and state standards, which provide the context in which you will be teaching science

- the content knowledge teachers need to feel confident in their ability to teach the required science and to provide a framework for developing quality science learning experiences for grades K–2 children

What Are the Big Ideas in Science?

Just as science processes are subdivided, science content, too, is organized into key concepts, which are the foremost ideas around which science is organized. Children can learn these key concepts as a consequence of their experiential inquiry. When you have a clear idea of the concepts you wish children to ascertain from an experience, children will be more apt to learn those concepts. It is important, therefore, that you be as well versed in the subject matter of science as possible. In addition, by knowing the basics of what your children need to know by the end of the second grade, you will be more confident in your teaching and feel less fearful of teaching science.

More than a decade ago, the National Center for Improving Science Education recommended that elementary schools design curricula that introduce nine scientific concepts. The nine concepts, the Big Ideas of science, are still relevant to today's elementary child:

Big Ideas in Science

- organization
- cause and effect
- systems
- scale
- models

- change
- structure and function
- variation
- diversity

1. **Organization.** Scientists have made the study of science manageable by organizing and classifying natural phenomena. For example, natural objects can be assembled in hierarchies (atoms, molecules, mineral, grains, rocks, strata, hills, mountains, and planets). Or, objects can be arranged according to their complexity (single-celled amoeba, sponges, and so on, to mammals). K–2 children can be introduced to this concept by sorting objects like leaves, shells, or rocks according to their characteristics.

2. **Cause and effect.** Nature behaves in predictable ways. Searching for explanations is the major activity of science; effects cannot occur without causes. Young children can learn about cause and effect by observing the effect that light, water, and warmth have on seeds and plants.

3. **Systems.** A system is a whole that is composed of parts arranged in an orderly manner according to some scheme or plan. In science, systems involve matter, energy, and information that move through defined pathways. The amount of matter, energy, and information, and the rate at which they are transferred through the pathways varies over time. Children begin to understand systems by tracking changes among the individual parts. Young children can learn about systems by studying the notion of balance—for example, by observing the movements and interactions in an aquarium ecosystem.

4. **Scale.** Scale refers to quantity, both relative and absolute. Thermometers, rulers, and weighing devices help children see that objects and energy vary in quantity. It is hard for children to understand that certain phenomena can exist only within fixed limits of size. Yet young children can begin to understand scale if they are asked, for instance, to imagine a mouse the size of an elephant. Would the mouse still have the same proportions if it were that large? What changes would have to occur in the elephant-sized mouse for it to function?

5. **Models.** We can create or design objects that represent other things. This is a hard concept for very young children. But young children can gain experience by building a model plane with paper or a car with toilet paper rolls.

6. **Change.** The natural world continually changes, although some changes may be too slow to observe. Rates of change vary. Children can be asked to observe changes in the position and apparent shape of the moon. Parents and children can track the position of the moon at the same time each night and draw pictures of the moon's changing shape to learn that change takes place during the lunar cycle. Children can also observe and

describe changes in the properties of water when it boils, melts, evaporates, freezes, or condenses.

7. **Structure and function.** A relationship exists between the way organisms and objects look (feel, smell, sound, and taste) and the things they do. Children can learn that skunks spray a bad odor to protect themselves. Children also can learn to infer what a mammal eats by studying its teeth or what a bird eats by studying the structure of its beak.

8. **Variation.** To understand the concept of organic evolution and the statistical nature of the world, children first need to understand that all organisms and objects have distinctive properties. Some of these properties are so distinctive that no continuum connects them—for example, living and nonliving things, or sugar and salt. In most of the natural world, however, the properties of organisms and objects vary continuously. Young children can learn about this concept by observing and arranging color by shades.

9. **Diversity.** This is the most obvious characteristic of the natural world. Even pre-K children know that there are many types of objects and organisms. Young children need to begin understanding that diversity in nature is essential for natural systems to survive. Children can explore and investigate a pond to learn that different organisms feed on different things (NSES, 1996).

What Concepts Should You Include in Your Curriculum?

The concepts selected as learning objectives for children should be based on your knowledge of the children and of the community in which they live, the nature of the larger society, and the main conceptual schemes found in science. Ask yourself the following questions as you begin to prepare for teaching:

- What experiences have the children had before coming to my class?

- In what things do they show an interest?

- What kinds of knowledge and skills do they need to function safely and effectively in the community in which they live and in the global community to which they belong?

- What will they need to know and be able to do to participate and succeed in the larger society?

- Which of the basic science concepts are relevant to them at this stage of their lives?

Questions such as these should be asked and answered as you develop your plan for teaching science.

Table 6.1 lists the topics selected by Texas, California, and New York State to reflect the national standards. The content standards of these three states closely align to each other and also to the national *Standards* with an emphasis on inquiry.

Table 6.1 Science Topics Covered by Each Grade, According to Texas, California, and New York Standards

Grade	California	New York	Texas
K	Physical science; Life science; Earth science; Investigation and experimentation	Exploring properties; Trees through the seasons; Animals	Components of natural world; Seasons and growth; Organisms and objects and their parts; Living versus nonliving organism
1	Physical science; Life science; Earth science; Investigation and experimentation	Properties of matter; Weather and seasons; Animal diversity	Components of natural world and resources; Things cause change; Basic needs of living things and interdependence; Living versus nonliving; Parts can be put together with other parts to do new things
2	Physical science; Life science; Earth science; Investigation and experimentation	Forces of motion; Plant diversity; Earth materials	Components and processes of natural world and resources; Change: Melting and evaporation, Weathering and pushing and pulling; Living versus nonliving; Needs of plants and animals/ Structure and function; Living organisms depend upon environment
3	Physical science; Life science; Earth science; Investigation and experimentation	Matter, energy; Simple machines; Plant and animal adaptations	Natural world: Rocks, soil, water and atmospheric gases; Change caused by force: Direction and position of objects pushed and pulled/Movement of Earth's surface; Magnetism and gravity; Organisms' needs, habitats, and competition within ecosystems

Teacher Activity: Your State Standards and Teaching Topics

Locate your state standards and list the topics you are required to teach at your grade level.

Grade _____

Topics that should be covered	Your level of comfort (5–1)
1. _____	_____
2. _____	_____
3. _____	_____
4. _____	_____
5. _____	_____
6. _____	_____

Next to each topic, write your level of comfort, with (5) being most comfortable (you know the content and have appropriate strategies for teaching the topic) and (1) being least comfortable (you need to understand content and develop teaching strategies).

How Do You Build an Effective Science Learning Environment?

This section is informed by the National Science Education program and system standards. You will find additional information at http://www.nap.edu/readingroom/books/nses/.

Creating an adequate environment for science teaching is a shared responsibility. Teachers lead the way in the design and use of resources, but school administrators, students, parents, and community members must meet their shared responsibility to ensure that the right resources are available to be used. Developing a schedule that allows time for science investigations needs the cooperation of all in the school. Acquiring materials requires the appropriation of funds. Maintaining scientific equipment is the shared responsibiity of children and teachers alike. Designing appropriate use of the scientific institutions and resources in the local community requires the participation of the school and those institutions and parents, teachers, and children.

Time, space, and materials are critical components of an effective science learning environment that promotes sustained inquiry and understanding.

Time

You should structure available time so that children are able to engage in extended investigations. Building scientific understanding takes time on a daily basis and over the long term. As you begin to plan, see if you can use blocks of time, interdisciplinary strategies, and field experiences to give children many opportunities to engage in serious scientific investigation as an integral part of their science learning. When considering how to structure available time, remember children need time to try out ideas, to make mistakes, to ponder, and to discuss with one another. As you schedule your time, provide adequate blocks of time for children to set up scientific equipment and carry out experiments, to go on field trips, or to reflect and share with each other. Allow children to work in varied groupings—alone, in pairs, in small groups, as a whole class—and on varied tasks, such as reading, conducting experiments, reflecting, writing, and sharing.

Space

Create a setting for children to work that is flexible and supportive of science inquiry. The arrangement of available space and furnishings in the classroom or laboratory influences the nature of the learning that takes place. You need regular, adequate space for science to allow children to work safely in groups of various sizes at various tasks, to maintain their work in progress, and to discuss and display their results.

Materials

Make the available science tools, materials, media, and technological resources accessible to children. Effective science teaching depends on the availability and organization of materials, equipment, media, and technology. An effective science learning environment requires a broad range of basic scientific materials, as well as specific tools for particular topics and learning experiences. As you plan for teaching you should select the most appropriate materials and make decisions about when, where, and how to make them accessible. Such decisions balance safety, proper use, and availability with the need for students to participate actively in designing experiments, selecting tools, and constructing apparatus, all of which are critical to the development of an understanding of inquiry. It is also important for children to learn how to access scientific information from Websites, books, periodicals, videos, data bases, electronic communication, and people with expert knowledge. As your children seek information, you need to help them evaluate and interpret the information they have acquired through those resources.

Safety

Always ensure a safe working environment. Safety is a fundamental concern in all experimental science. You must know and apply the necessary safety regulations in the storage, use, and care of the materials used by children. You also need to adhere to safety rules and guidelines that are established by national organizations such as the American Chemical Society (ACS) and the Occupational Safety and Health Administration (OSHA), as well as by local and state regulatory agencies. It is critical that at the beginning, you teach children how to engage safely in investigations inside and outside the classroom. You need to consider allergic reactions as you plan teaching materials and only allow children to taste materials if you have signed parental approval.

Involve Children

Involve young children in designing the learning environment. As part of challenging children to take responsibility for their learning, you could involve them in the design and management of the learning environment. Even the youngest child can and should participate in discussions and decisions about using time and space for work. For example, they can come to consensus about the location of the science corner or the aquarium. With this sharing comes responsibility for care of space and resources. As students pursue their inquiries, they need access to resources and a voice in determining what is needed. The more independently children can access what they need, the more they can take responsibility for their own work. Children are also invaluable in identifying resources in their community (NSES, 1996).

How Can You Set Up Your Classroom for Science?

Your physical setting will be dependent on your location, the economics of your community, and the importance that has been placed on science in the school and district. You might be in an urban school in which you cannot leave anything in your classroom and have to bring your supplies in daily, or at the other extreme, you might be in a very wealthy district or school with a room large enough to accommodate a science center and ongoing experiments. You might even have a room designated to science. Whatever your circumstances, you can teach science. I have watched teachers make science come alive in schools without walls, using materials they pull out of their handbags. I have also seen science taught in classrooms that have better science materials than some teacher training programs. Here are some ideas of what you can include in your room:

1. **Why board.** This is a prominent board on which you write children's "Why" questions.

2. **Science word wall.** Some words to include are: *science, scientists, problem, materials, procedure, observations, animals, plants,* etc. Other words can be added as topics are taught. (For example, a lesson on animals may include the words *living, nonliving, insects,* and *mammals.*)

3. **Science library.** Start collecting science books (fiction and nonfiction). Have children bring in books from their collections to donate to the classroom.

4. **Science materials.** Below is a list of basic science materials. (See *Science Stories* by Janice Koch (2005), for a complete suggested materials list.) You can purchase materials from discount or dollar stores or party stores or check online at www.discountschoolsupply.com or http://edushop. edu4kids.com/catalog/default.php; for a listing of free or inexpensive science resources, check http://amasci.com/edu_free_sci.html or nsta.org.

   - set of hand lenses

   - balance scales

   - measuring cups and spoons (in metric and standard measures)

   - assortment of pine cones, acorns, seeds from different plants

   - animal antlers and bones, fossils and rock collections, seashells

   - fish bowl with goldfish (no heater is needed; fish live a long time.)

   - rabbits, hamsters, guinea pigs, lizards, or hermit crabs (These pets are easy to take care of, and children love to take them home on vacations.) Remember: Get parental approval first and check with parents about allergies before bringing pets into the classroom.

   - ant farm or butterfly garden (Purchase caterpillars in the spring; children can watch them go through metamorphosis.)

   - basic cooking supplies (salt, sugar, cooking oil, baking soda, flour)

   - containers (beakers, bottles, plastic cups, funnels)

   - Epsom salts (used to show scientific concepts like evaporation, dissolving, texture)

   - other supplies—potting soil, balloons, drinking straws, scale, flashlights, string, magnets, thermometers

5. Science corner. A science corner is a special interactive corner in the classroom devoted to science where

- science materials are located

- there is usually a large table for working

- the materials on the table are well organized so that items are accessible

- both formal and informal science teaching and learning can take place

Teacher Activity: Science Corners

Science corners should be changed often to meet the needs of the students and the curriculum. Your science corner should focus on encouraging learning through discovery. Science corners are not only the responsibility of the teacher. Children can also

- contribute items to the science corner

- participate in taking care of a science corner in their classroom

- rotate as the designated "science resource person" in charge of the corner

Before setting up your science center, as part of your plan for teaching, answer the following questions:

- What do you see as the value of a science corner?

_____

- How would you utilize a science corner in your classroom?

_____

- What materials and resources would you include?

_____

- Where can you find materials for science teaching?

_____

- Do you have a budget for science materials? What is the budget? Who purchases materials? How many months in advance do you need your list of required materials? Are there science kits available in your school?

_____

- Is there a science room or closet with materials from previous years?

_____

If you do not know the answers to some of these questions, you should talk to your Principal. You need this information as you begin to plan for teaching.

Teacher Activity: Final Reflection

Many of you teach science in a "regular" classroom. As you develop your plan for teaching science, think about the following:

- How can you adapt your current classroom to create an effective science learning environment?
- What do you need to change or add to your room to accommodate science teaching?
- Would you have to change your teaching schedule? Can you change it?
- What issues arise in science that might not occur in your other subject areas?
- Where can you store your science materials?

Take-Away Thought

When young children come to you in kindergarten through second grade, they are filled with "why" questions; they are emerging as scientists. Your goal is to help them maintain their interest and curiosity about science.

7

Resources You Can Use in Your Science Teaching

Focus Questions

- What resources are available for teaching K–2 science?

- Where can you find information on these resources?

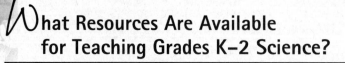

What Resources Are Available for Teaching Grades K–2 Science?

The school science program must extend beyond the walls of the school to the resources of the community. Your children's education should not be limited to what goes on within the walls of the school building. The classroom is a limited environment. As an effective teacher, you should identify and use resources outside the school. The physical environment in and around the school can be used as a living laboratory for the study of natural phenomena. Whether your school is located in a densely populated urban area, a sprawling suburb, a small town, or a rural area, the environment can and should be used as a resource for science study. Working with others in your school and with the community, you can build these resources into your work with children.

In this exercise, explore the science teaching resources that are available for use in your day-to-day teaching.

Teacher Activity: Your Available Resources for Teaching Science

List the resources you think you will have available for teaching grades K–2 science.

_____

_____

_____

_____

_____

_____

_____

_____

_____

_____

Let us take a look at some of the available resources for teaching science to young children.

You

The first and most critical resource that you have for teaching science is you—your willingness to be adventurous, to be flexible, and to use everything around you as a science teaching resource for your children. Science is a difficult subject to teach, and you need to gather all the resources you can find to help you in your teaching of science that children will find meaningful and that does not stifle their endless "why" questions. When they leave you and move up to the next level, their scientific selves must continue to emerge.

To many K–2 teachers, science is an entity that they do not know; neither do they know how to reply to all the questions that children pose to them. You will find that the more you teach science, the more you learn. Do not resist teaching science because you do not know the content. In Appendix 2, you will find some essential content that will help you begin to develop an understanding of the content needed to teach science to K–2 children. As teachers, we sometimes feel that we are supposed to have all the answers. I vividly recall one class, during my graduate work, when I was preparing to be a science teacher, when my K–6 methods professor wrote on the board the following: "Wait time" and "I do not know. Let's find out." He proceeded to tell us that these would be the strategies we would use most frequently in our daily teaching. He was so correct. As a teacher, I have found that I am most successful if I give my children time to reflect before responding to my questions, and if I foster an environment in my class in which I work with children to find answers to their questions, rather than supplying them with the answer. We learn together. Children become the masters of their own learning. Throughout this book, there are strategies you can use to help your children find answers to their "why" questions. You want to give the children the best start in life. In the early years, you want them to begin to develop critical thinking and life skills. These are the skills that are basic in the development of scientific literacy. Good science education fosters to scientific literacy, which in turn equates to critical thinking. As their first teacher, you have the development of their critical thinking capacity in your hands. However, you are not alone. The following sections explore the resources you can use to assist you in this task.

Scientists

If we want our children to become scientists, we need to provide them with role models so that they can begin from an early age to identify with scientists and to realize that they too can aspire to being a scientist. Our nation's communities have many specialists, including those in transportation, health care delivery, communications, computer technologies, music, art, cooking, mechanics, and many other fields that have scientific aspects. Specialists are often available as resources for classes and for individual children. Many communities have access to science centers and museums as well as to the science communities in higher education, national laboratories, and industry. These can contribute greatly to the understanding of science and encourage children to further their interests outside of school.

You are working with very young children in grades K–2; this is the age when we should begin to have them interact with scientists to have them begin to find answers to questions such as

- What do scientists do?
- Who are scientists?
- What do scientists look like?

This is when you should begin to bring scientists from the community into the classroom and expose your children to the day-to-day life of a scientist. You want children to begin to realize that scientists are normal people, scientists are "cool." This is the age when children begin to talk about what they want to be when they grow up and you want them to include "being a scientist" as one of their aspirations. They can begin to think about being a nurse, pharmacist, doctor, dentist, medical technician, laboratory researcher, physicist, chemist, environmental scientist. Remember: one way of having children include these images in their dreams is to expose them to real-life role models. In the "Draw a Scientist" activity (see Chapter 1) you were reminded that scientists don't always wear lab coats and that they can be women or minorities.

Teacher Activity: What Scientists Are Available in Your Community?

1. Make a list of the scientists you would like to come to your classroom. Include their contact information and what you perceive they can contribute to your children. You can use your local yellow pages or the Web to locate them.

Name	Contact Information	Scientific Contribution
_____	_____	_____
_____	_____	_____
_____	_____	_____
_____	_____	_____
_____	_____	_____

(continued on next page)

Teacher Activity: What Scientists Are Available in Your Community? (cont.)

2. Once you have completed this list, have your children write the questions they would like to ask the scientist on their question board. Have the scientists answer those questions during their visit to your class.

Nonformal Institutions

The world outside of the classroom can provide useful stimuli for responding to questions your children have asked and for getting them to ask new questions. Schools are essentially places that provide the opportunity for intense, conscious, systematic, and formalized learning. The following guidelines for visits to these institutions were originally generated by the U.S. DoE. For additional information you should consult their Website: http://www.ed.gov/pubs/ parents/science/index.html. You should also visit the Website: http://www. yallaa.com/directory/reference/museums/science/ of the education programs listed in the references for site opportunities and guidelines for your grade level. Nonformal science settings provide your children with opportunities to develop their scientific literacy outside the walls of the school. Nonformal sites encompass unique settings such as

- museums
- zoos
- botanical gardens
- rivers
- parks
- playgrounds

In such settings, information, stimulation, and experiences are provided almost entirely through objects, their interpretative display, and, in many cases, through the manipulation of these objects. If activities at these sites are well structured, they can go a long way toward providing your children with levels of knowledge and awareness in science to help them meet the requirements of the *National Science Education Standards* and the *Benchmarks*. You can use fieldtrips in teaching the national and state standards, the Big Ideas, and your curriculum. Your field trips should extend and reinforce what is taking place in your classroom. Nonformal sites, with their abundance of resources, provide opportunities to reinforce the formalized learning of the school system with concrete experiences. They can present phenomena in the form of exhibits that are interactive, with a focus on enabling visitors to explore, manipulate, and experiment. They provide a venue for your children to see animals or plants that you talk about in school or that they see in books or TV. You can include in your curriculum visits to museums, zoos, parks, botanical gardens, and even to the area around your school. Try to focus on science around you and use the environment to teach science. Remember, science can be learned in many places and environments.

Zoos. Almost all children enjoy a trip to the zoo. We can use zoos to encourage their interest in the natural world and to introduce them to animal diversity.

Guessing games can help them understand structure and function. Here are some sample questions:

- Why do you think the seal has flippers? (The seal uses flippers to swim through the water.)
- Why do you think the gibbons have such long and muscular arms? (Their arms help them swing through the trees.)
- Why does the armadillo have a head that looks like it's covered with armor, as well as a body that's covered with small, bony plates? (The armor and the bony plates protect it from being attacked by predators.)
- Why is the snake the same green color as the leaves in which it spends most of its time? (As snakes evolved, the green ones did not get eaten as quickly.)

Children can learn about organization by seeing related animals. Here are some ideas:

- Have them compare the sizes of legs, feet, ears, claws, feathers, or scales of various animals.
- Ask such questions as Does the lion look like your cat at home? How are they the same? How are they different? or Why does the giraffe have such a long neck?

Planning a trip to the zoo for a class of twenty-five kindergarteners or first-graders can be a daunting experience, but it is manageable and can be lots of fun for you and your children. Here are a few suggestions to help make your visit worthwhile:

1. **Discuss expectations with your children ahead of time.** What do they think they'll find at the zoo? Very young or insecure children may go to the zoo with a more positive attitude if they are assured that it has food stands, water fountains, and bathrooms and that their parents can come along.

2. **Don't try to see everything in one visit.** Zoos are such busy places that they can overwhelm youngsters, particularly K–2 children. Before your class visit, you should visit the zoo and select the animals you want your students to see.

3. **Try to visit zoos at off times or hours.** Visiting in winter, for example, or very early in the morning or late afternoon provides some peace and quiet and gives children unobstructed views of the animals. Try to schedule visits when the zoo is quiet and also when parents can accompany your class.

4. **Look for special exhibits and facilities for children.** Such exhibits as family learning labs or petting zoos provide children the opportunity to touch and examine animals and engage in projects specially designed for them. For example, at the Please Touch Museum in Philadelphia, children can learn about dinosaurs by doing a dinosaur dig.

5. **Plan follow-up activities and projects.** A child who particularly liked the flamingos and ducks may enjoy building a bird house for her backyard. One who liked the turtle may enjoy building a papier-mâché turtle. One who enjoyed the fish might want to start a classroom aquarium.

Museums. Museums are designed today to interest visitors of all ages. Science and technology museums, natural history museums, and children's museums can be found in many middle-sized and smaller communities such as Toledo (Ohio), Monsey (New York), and Worland (Wyoming), as well as in large metropolitan areas like Los Angeles, Chicago, and New York City.

Museums vary in quality. If possible, seek out those that provide opportunities for hands-on activities. Look for museums with

- levers to pull
- bubbles to blow
- lights to switch on
- buttons to push
- animals to stroke
- experiments to do

Natural history museums sometimes have hands-on rooms where children can stroke everything from lizards to Madagascan hissing cockroaches to frogs.

Many museums offer special science classes. Look for special science feature movie theaters. Some in-museum theaters enable visitors to see movies projected on a giant screen on subjects ranging from space launches to deep sea diving. The sounds and sights of the experience are extremely realistic and appealing to young children.

If you are unfamiliar with museums in your area, consult a librarian, the Yellow Pages of your telephone book, a local guidebook, or the local newspapers, which often list special exhibits; of course, you can also check their Website online. In the references for this chapter, there is a list of Websites for national museums. You can even take your children for a virtual visit to some museums; for example, the American Museum of Natural History in New York has a Website that takes you through their exhibits.

The tips for visiting the zoo are also helpful when you visit museums or other community facilities.

Aquariums. Aquariums enable youngsters to see everything from starfish to electric eels. Children particularly enjoy feeding times. Remember to call ahead to find out when the penguins, sharks, and other creatures get fed. Check for special shows with sea lions and dolphins.

Farms. A visit to a farm makes a wonderful field trip for young children. It can provide experiences in life science and technology. If you don't know a farmer, call the closest 4-H Club, your Cooperative Extension, or a master

gardener for a referral. Consider dairy farms as well as vegetable, poultry, pig, and tree farms.

On a dairy farm, children can see cows close up, view silos, and learn what cows eat. Your children can find out from the farmer answers to such questions as

- Up to what age do calves drink only milk?

- When do they add other items to their diets? What are they?

- Why are the various foods a cow eats nutritious?

A visit to a farm also enables children to identify the difference between calves, heifers, and cows; to watch the cows being milked; to see farm equipment; to sit on tractors; and to ask questions about how tractors work.

If you visit a vegetable farm, encourage your children to look at the crops and ask questions about how they grow. If your children grew up in an urban area, they may have no idea what apples or potatoes or beans look like growing in a field.

Let the children discover what farmers do with their organic waste. Is there a composter on site? How does it work? Maybe you can do composting at your school.

Where Can You Find Information on These Resources?

Science learning and, ultimately, scientific literacy for all depend on the teaching that occurs both in schools and in nonformal settings. As we move toward the attainment of scientific literacy for all, it is imperative that we recognize and utilize the media, industry, education programs, nonformal science centers, museums, and other science learning outlets as valuable segments of our nation's science education infrastructure. As a K–2 teacher, you need to develop the ability to use the nonformal context to teach elementary science. These sites can provide immense support as you implement your science teaching in schools that have a paucity of resources but that are located close to nonformal sites that house an abundant, yet often untapped, set of resources. In the reference section, you will find examples of nonformal institutions you can use as a resource in your teaching. The listing also includes some international locations you might find useful in your science teaching. Visit their Websites to get information about their education programs and the availability of virtual tours or field trips.

Teacher Activity: Nonformal Resources

1. List the accessible nonformal institutions within walking distance or in close proximity of your school. Include their contact information and what you perceive they can contribute to your children's education.

   _____

   _____

   _____

   _____

   _____

   _____

2. List the nonformal institutions that will accommodate grades K–2 children.

   _____

   _____

   _____

   _____

3. Investigate and list what you need to do to take your children to the site.

   _____

   _____

   _____

   _____

4. What do these sites offer K–2 children?

   _____

   _____

   _____

   _____

5. Contact them and get their brochures, or visit their Websites.

   Keep all this information in your folder, since you will need to refer to it as you develop your plan for teaching.

Parents

Parents are the first teachers of their children and usually are very keen on being involved in the education of their K–2 child. You need to foster their desire to continue this involvement and invite them into the classroom or on field trips. They are the major influences on their children during their early years, so you want them to be involved in and excited about what you are doing in school. Plan family science nights in which you share with them the activities you are doing with their children. Do some activities with them. Have them relive the excitement of discovery.

Use parents or community members as judges for your science fairs. This shows children that their parents and the community value science education. At this level, judging should include asking children about their exhibits and giving them stars for their participation. The interaction with adults gives a sense of importance to the science fair and fosters continued interest and excitement in science.

Invite the community to have your children visit places around the community that use science (dry cleaners, restaurants, hair salons, water department, parks, etc.). When children see science in places they frequent, they will have a better grasp of the importance of science in their daily lives. They will begin to realize that science surrounds them and is worthwhile. Parents and members of the community are usually more than willing to come into the classroom and bring an experiment or talk to the children about science in their lives.

Teacher Activity: Parents as Resources

On the first day of school, or earlier, if practical, send a letter out to parents telling them about what you want to do in science and enlisting their help. Ask for volunteers for field trips, classroom visits, science nights, and other activities you have planned.

Sample Letter to Parents

Dear Parents or Guardians:

Welcome to first grade. My name is _____ and I am excited about the upcoming school year and the possibilities for learning that await my new class.

First grade is an important time for the academic and social development of your children. This year, we will be spending a considerable amount of time working on their reading, writing, and math skills. Additionally, we will be exploring the worlds of social studies and science with discussions, readings, activities, and experiments. My goal is to help your child develop a love of learning through exploration of their interests and further development/improvement of their skills in all areas of the curriculum.

(continued on next page)

Teacher Activity: Parents as Resources (continued)

You will be receiving monthly updates about what your child is learning in class. Additionally, you may receive notes about important events or activities throughout the year.

In order to make this year successful, not only does your child need your support at home, but also in the classroom. I would like to enhance the learning experience with a number of hands-on activities and experiments in science. If you have any supplies at home that you could donate from the suggested list below, or anything else you think we could use, please send them in with your child or drop them off at the front desk with room number ___ on the front.

- glue
- scissors
- string
- butcher paper
- magnets
- boxes
- quick-growing seeds
- leaves/plants
- cups (paper/plastic)
- small mirrors
- plastic bags
- empty bottles (soda, juice)
- plastic spoons
- aquarium
- fossils
- rocks

I would like to thank you in advance for your help. This is going to be a great year. I look forward to meeting both you and your child this fall. Please do not hesitate to contact me by email or phone if you have any questions or other concerns.

Sincerely,

_____

Note: The list of materials needed will vary, based on the needs of your school district.

Use parents' responses to your letter to make up a database of available parents, and remember to enlist their help as you teach science. You should include their name, address, phone numbers, expertise, and availability. You could also ask them if they are available to accompany their child on field trips.

Journals and Books

You could examine the following journals for very interesting activities that will engage your emerging scientists:

- *Science and Children* (National Science Teachers' Association; NSTA)
- *Journal of Elementary Science Education* (JESE)

As a teacher, you should consider membership in NSTA, since this association provides numerous teaching resources and activities through their journals, Website, and national and regional meetings.

Here are three books that you may want to add to your resource collection:

1. *Ten-Minute Field Trips*, 3rd ed., by Helen Ross Russell (1998).
2. *Teaching Green—The Elementary Years: Hands-On Learning in Grades K–5*, edited by Tim Grant and Gail Littlejohn (2005).
3. *Into the Field: A Guide to Locally Focused Teaching*, by Leslie Clare Walker (2005).

Internet

The Internet has evolved into an excellent resource for teaching science. You can find useful ideas for teaching science at all levels. Web resources promote:

- active learning
- more hands-on experiences
- creativity
- engaged children
- enhanced lessons

An excellent Website is TeachersTV.com, a British-based site that provides content, activities, strategies, and useful teaching tips for K–12 science.

Tables 7.1 and 7.2 list Websites helpful for planning activities for teaching grade K–2 science.

Teacher Activity: Integrating the Web into Your Teaching

Science content for your grade	Relevant websites that contain materials you can use
_____	_____
_____	_____
_____	_____
_____	_____
_____	_____
_____	_____
_____	_____
_____	_____

Table 7.1 General Websites for Any Grade, Children and Teachers

- Exploratorium Website—Live webcasts with scientists and museum tour guides
  http://www.exploratorium.edu/index.html
- Website with small useful science modules on a variety of science topics
  http://www.bbc.co.uk/schools/
- Magic School Bus virtual tours
  http://place.scholastic.com/magicschoolbus/tour/home.htm
- Foss website: Each module has information on the topics: pictures, other websites, movies, and interactive games for kids as well as Parent/Teacher info
  http://www.fossweb.com/modulesK-2/index.html
- Brain Pop—videos and quizzes on science topics
  http://www.brainpop.com/science/seeall/
- For teachers: lets you customize your grade and subject and it gives you a list of great resources
  http://www.pbs.org/teachers/sciencetech/
- Bill Nye's interactive Website
  http://www.billnye.com/
- British-based Website
  TeachersTV.com

Source: This list was developed by two NYC elementary teachers, Hallie Saltz and Lindsey Webster, using materials modified from _Teaching Science as Investigation_ by H. Moyer, J. J. K. Hackett, and S.A. Everett (Upper Saddle River, NJ: Prentice Hall, 2006).

$\mathcal{T}able\ 7.2$ Suggested Websites for Use in Grades K–2

Unit	Websites
Unit 1	
1. Exploring Properties: What are the properties of matter that determine observable characteristics?	1. Sorting materials: http://www.bbc.co.uk/schools/scienceclips/ages/5_6/ sorting_using_mate.shtml How Earth materials are used: http://www.fossweb.com/modulesK-2/PebblesSandandSilt/index.html
2. Animal Diversity: How do variations in form and function help animals meet their needs?	2. Find an insect around the land and a pond: http://www.fossweb.com/modulesK-2/PebblesSandandSilt/index.html
3. Animal and Plant adaptations: How are animals and plants suited for their environment?	3. Watch plants grow—change light and watering, and see how that changes the growth process: http://www.bbc.co.uk/schools/scienceclips/ages/5_6/ growing_plants.shtml Additional: Magic School Bus Tours, Games, and more: http://place.scholastic.com/magicschoolbus/tour/tour.htm?animals
Unit 2	
1. Seasons: What are observable changes in weather?	1. Dress the bear for the weather: http://www.fossweb.com/modulesK-2/AirandWeather/index.html
2. Weather: What forces shape our planet?	2. Make a weather station: learn about wind, air pressure, moisture, and temperature: http://www.miamisci.org/hurricane/
3. Earth, Moon, and Sun: What are the relationships between the three?	3. Interactive science physical processes, including circuits, forces of motion, Earth, Sun, and Moon: http://www.bbc.co.uk/schools/ks2bitesize/science/activities/ earth_sun_moon.shtml
Unit 3	
1. Forces and Motion: How do forces affect objects?	1. Build a roller coaster. Learn how things move: http://www.fossweb.com/modulesK-2/BalanceandMotion/index.html
2. Matter and its properties: How do you differentiate objects based on physical properties?	2. Learn how wood is processed into paper: http://www.fossweb.com/modulesK-2/WoodandPaper/index.html

(continued on next page)

Table 7.2 Suggested Websites for Use in Grades K–2 (continued)

Unit	Websites
Unit 3 (continued	
3. Forces and Energy: How do forces interact with matter?	3. Properties of magnets and magnetic materials: http://www.bbc.co.uk/schools/ks2bitesize/science/activities/magnets_springs.shtml
Unit 4	
1. Life Processes and Interactions: What are the differences between living and nonliving things?	1. States of matter: Learn how substances change state to state http://www.fossweb.com/modulesK–2/solidsandliquids/index
2. Forces and Energy: How do magnetism, sound, light, and heat interact with matter (melting and heating)?	2. Learn about the properties of sound. Build an orchestra: http://www.carnegiehall.org/article/explore_and_learn/art_online_resources_listening_adventures.html Learn what objects give off light: http://www.bbc.co.uk/schools/scienceclips/ages/5_6/light_dark.shtml
3. Properties of Water: How do properties of water affect interactions with other objects?	3. Water Science: Investigating the water cycle: http://ga.water.usgs.gov/edu Properties of water: Life on Earth http://www.fossweb.com/modules3-6/water/index.html
Unit 5	
1. Animal and Plant Characteristics: What are the basic parts and types of plants and animals?	1. Plants and animals in their local environment: http://www.bbc.co.uk/schools/scienceclips/ages/6_7/plants_animals_env.shtml Identify insects around land and ponds: http://www.fossweb.com/modulesK-2/insects/index.html
2. Plant Diversity: How do variations in form and function help plants meet their needs?	2. Identify the organisms that live in trees, swamps, and deserts: http://www.fossweb.com/modulesK-2/trees/index.html
3. Habitat Study: How do plants and animals interact in a pond ecosystem?	3. Watch the growth of a plant changing light and water: http://www.bbc.co.uk/schools/scienceclips/ages/5_6/growing_plants.shtml Build your own fish online and release it into the virtual fish tank: http://www.virtualfishtank.com/main.html

Source: Adapted from *Teaching Science as Investigations*, by Richard H. Moyer, Jay K. Hackett, and Susan A. Everett (Upper Saddle River, NJ: Prentice Hall, 2006) by two NYC elementary teachers, Hallie Saltz and Lindsey Webster.

Education Programs

Many institutions have extensive Websites and offer virtual fieldtrips that can be integrated into your teaching. In the references for this chapter, you will find a listing of some of these programs.

Take-Away Thought

Resources for teaching science are everywhere. You just need to know where to look.

Do not use lack of money as an excuse for not teaching science.

Developing Your Plan for Teaching Science

Focus Questions

- Where am I in my development as a science teacher?

- Where am I going in my science teaching practice?

- How do I plan to be an effective science teacher?

- How will I know when I have arrived at my best level of practice?

As you progress through the exercises and activities in this chapter and begin to plan learning experiences for your young children, you should be developing an awareness of your own level of preparedness for the task ahead.

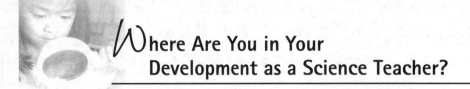

Where Are You in Your Development as a Science Teacher?

Initial Reflection: Assessing Where You Are

Whatever your role in science teaching, these are some questions to think about as you develop the phases of your plan for each lesson within your curriculum.

1. Under what conditions do you currently teach (or plan to teach) science?

   _____

2. Is your curriculum text or kit based? Or a combination of both?

   _____

3. Has your school district adopted a specific curriculum?

   _____

4. Has your school developed its own curriculum?

   _____

5. Has your school adopted a specific textbook?

   _____

6. Are you expected to use the textbook as written?

   _____

7. Are you expected to develop your own curriculum?

   _____

8. Do you have a science cluster teacher (or a teacher specifically dedicated to science teaching)?

   _____

Earlier, we used the analogy of going on a journey. To continue that analogy, if you do not know where you are in your development as a science teacher, then it is difficult to plan your future journey to your best level of science teaching practice. While answering the question, "Where am I in my development as a science teacher?" you should ask and seek answers to the question, Where are my children? Consider these questions:

- What do you need to do to prepare all your children for the journey to scientific literacy?
- What is the range of intellectual abilities in the class?
- What about their emotional development?
- What do they currently know?
- What did they do in the previous grade?
- What experiences do they bring from home?

Remember that in your class, you will have different intellectual abilities, as well as significant differences in emotional and motor skill development.

Where Are You Going in Your Science Teaching Practice?

Each state has interpreted the national *Standards* and *Benchmarks* to develop their own state standards and frameworks. In turn, many districts have developed their own standards, which are often translated into individual school standards. (See Figure 8.1.) These are the standards that you use in your own classroom when you begin teaching to achieve scientific literacy for all of your children.

Figure 8.1 The *Standards* and the *Benchmarks*

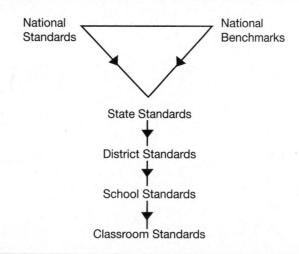

All of the previous chapters have been leading up to this one in which you plan for the journey to scientific literacy for all your children. The information you collected in Chapters 1–7 are essential for planning to teach science in your classroom. In your planning, you need to decide which conditions are most conducive to learning in your contextual framework. Remember, there is no single format or strategy that meets the needs of all communities and the teaching and learning styles of all teachers and children. You have the opportunity to develop your own format based on the needs of your children and your ability to meet those needs. No curriculum developer can produce the optimum teaching strategy for your classroom. Only you can do this.

As you develop your curriculum, you should assimilate ideas presented in this book, in curriculum material you have seen, as well as in Websites and material developed by your state or elsewhere. Collect and use as many resources as you can find, then adapt them to make your own curriculum for use in your current classroom. Remember also that your plans must always be flexible, since you do not know what questions will surface as you engage your children in new experiences. Their questions and interest might take your lesson in a completely different direction. Always be prepared for the unpredictable. You should be constantly engaged in the task of decision making as you sift, sort and decide on meaningful experiences for your children.

State Standards

In Appendix 1, you will find the *National Science Education Standards* and the *Benchmarks*. These are the guides that each state uses to make decisions about the content of their K–12 science requirements.

Locate the national standards and copy them for your personal use. You should store them in your folder. Try this Website: http://www.nap.edu/readingroom/books/nses/overview.html#organization

$\mathcal{T}$eacher $\mathcal{A}$ctivity: Mapping the State Standards

1. Go to your state Website, find the state K–2 science standards (sometimes called frameworks) and include in your folder. If you have problems locating your state Website, you can check this link: http://edstandards.org/standards.html. (This site, developed by Charles Hill, has been on the Net since August 1995, first with the Putnam Valley School District and now the Wappingers Central School District—both in upstate New York.)

2. Review both national and state standards for similarities and differences. Are there any major differences? Does one reflect the other?

_____

_____

_____

_____

_____

Study these documents carefully and see if you can make connections between them. Read the documents and highlight key words that point to the need for activity-based instruction. Explore your state, district, or city Websites for science lessons and activities.

City and District Standards

As you research further, you will find that many cities and districts have developed their own standards or scope and sequence. For example, New York City recently developed a scope and sequence for K–8.

$\mathcal{T}$eacher $\mathcal{A}$ctivity: Mapping the District Standards

Go to your district Website, find the relevant standards, and include them in your folder.

Tables 8.1, 8.2, and 8.3 show scope and sequence delineated by New York City for grades K–2.

Table 8.1 Scope and Sequence for Kindergarten Science

Unit 1 Exploring Properties	Unit 2 Trees Through the Seasons	Unit 3 Animals
How do we observe and describe objects?	*What are some changes we see in trees during the year?*	*What are animals?*
Observe and, using all of the appropriate senses, describe physical properties of objects. • size, shape, texture, weight, color, etc. • determine whether objects are alike or different	Identify the basic needs of organisms to live and thrive. • needs of plants to live and thrive (e.g., air, water, light) • needs of living things to grow and change	Identify the basic needs of organisms to live and thrive. • needs of animals to live and thrive (e.g., air, water, food, shelter) • needs of living things to grow and change
Observe and describe physical properties of objects using appropriate tools. • hot/cold (thermometer) • weight (pan balance) • measurement (nonstandard units), including bigger/smaller, more/less, capacity of liquids	Observe and compare the different structures that enable each plant to live and thrive. • roots, leaves, stems, flowers, seeds	Observe and compare the different structures that enable each animal to live and thrive. • wings, legs, fins, eyes, nose, ears, tongue, skin, claws, etc.
Observe, describe, and identify the properties of materials (e.g., wood, plastic, metal).	Observe adaptations of plants. Plants respond to changes in the environment, including seasonal changes such as: • leaves falling in autumn and forming in springtime • flowers blooming	Make clear that nonliving things do not live and thrive.
Sort or group objects according to their properties. • texture, color, shape, etc. • sink or float		Recognize that living things have offspring and that offspring closely resemble their parents. • dogs/puppies, cats/kittens, cows/calves, ducks/ducklings, frogs/tadpoles Observe physical animal characteristics that are influenced by changing environmental conditions. • nest building, hibernation, migration

Table 8.2 Scope and Sequence for First-Grade Science

Unit 1 Properties of Matter	Unit 2 Weather and Seasons	Unit 3 Animal Diversity
What are some properties of solids, liquids, and gases?	*What are some of the changes we notice between seasons?*	*How are animals alike and different?*
Observe and describe the three states of matter. • Liquids take the shape of the containers they are in. • Air does not have a definite shape. • Solids have a definite shape.	Observe and describe weather conditions that occur during each season.	Identify, describe, and compare the physical structures of animals (e.g., body coverings, sensory organs, appendages, beaks).
Observe and describe how water evaporates when left in an open container (e.g., liquid water changes into gas as it moves into the air).	Observe, measure, record, and compare weather data throughout the year (e.g., cloud cover, cloud types, wind speed and direction, precipitation) by using thermometers, anemometers, wind vanes, and rain gauges.	Identify, in animals, the relationship between the physical structures and the functions of those structures (e.g., obtaining food and water, protection, movement, support).
Observe that the material(s) of which an object is made determines some specific properties of the object (sinking/ flotation, solubility).	Compare temperatures in different locations (e.g., inside, outside, in the sun, in the shade) and compare day and night temperatures.	Compare and contrast the physical characteristics in animals.
Predict, observe, and examine different substances to determine their ability to mix with water (e.g., oil and water, sugar and water, sand and water).	Illustrate and describe how the sun appears to move during the day.	Describe how physical traits help a species to survive (e.g., a giraffe's neck, a turtle's shell).
Use tools, such as hand lenses, rulers, thermometers, and balances, to observe and measure the properties of materials.	Illustrate and describe how the moon changes appearance over time (phases of the moon).	Observe how animals grow and change in predictable ways. • Animals closely resemble their parents and other individuals in their species. • Some traits of living things have been inherited (e.g., number of limbs).

(continued on next page)

Table 8.2   Scope and Sequence for First-Grade Science (continued)

Unit 1 Properties of Matter	Unit 2 Weather and Seasons	Unit 3 Animal Diversity
What are some properties of solids, liquids, and gases?	*What are some of the changes we notice between seasons?*	*How are animals alike and different?*
Test objects to determine whether they sink or float. • different materials (plastic, rubber, etc.) • different shapes • boat design	Describe the 24-hour day/night cycle (time).	Describe animal life cycles and life spans (e.g., baby/adult, puppy to dog).
Observe and describe the change of objects when placed in different environments. • hot and cold • lighting and shadows • color • wet and dry	Observe and record the changes in the sun's and other stars' position and the moon's appearance relative to time of day and month, and note the pattern of this change.	
	Recognize that the sun's energy warms the air.	

Table 8.3   Scope and Sequence for Second-Grade Science

Unit 1. Forces and Motion	Unit 2. Earth Materials	Unit 3. Plant Diversity
What causes objects to move?	*What materials make up the Earth?*	*How are plants alike and different?*
Observe and describe the position of an object relative to another object (over, under, on top of, next to).	Observe and describe the basic properties and components of soil. • living components • nonliving components	Identify and compare the physical structures of a variety of plant parts (seeds, leaves, stems, flowers, roots).

(continued on next page)

Table 8.3 Scope and Sequence for Second-Grade Science (continued)

Unit 1. Forces and Motion	Unit 2. Earth Materials	Unit 3. Plant Diversity
What causes objects to move?	*What materials make up the Earth?*	*How are plants alike and different?*
Identify a force as push or a pull.	Investigate different types of soil according to: • color • texture • materials • capacity to retain water	Observe and describe how plants grow and change in predictable ways. • Plants closely resemble their parents and other individuals of their species. • Some traits of living things have been inherited (e.g., color of flower).
Demonstrate how the position or direction of an object can be changed by pushing or pulling (forces and motion). • Change the direction of objects by pushing and pulling using blocks, ramps, cars, ball, inclined plane.	Explore how erosion and deposition are the result of interactions between air, wind, water, and land.	Observe plant life cycles and life spans.
Identify gravity as a force that pulls objects down. • the balance scale • balance and the center of gravity	Observe and describe the physical properties of rocks (size, shape, color, presence of fossils).	Observe that plants reproduce from • seeds, bulbs, and cuttings
Observe and describe how the force of gravity can affect objects through air, liquids, and solids.	Compare and sort rocks by size, color, luster, texture, patterns, hardness/softness. Make clear that nonliving things can be human created or naturally occurring.	Describe the basic needs of plants. • light, air, water, soil (nutrients) Describe the basic life functions of plants. • grow • take in nutrients • reproduce Observe that plants respond to changes in their environment (e.g., the leaves of some green plants change position as the direction of light changes; the parts of some plants undergo seasonal changes that enable the plant to grow; seeds to germinate, and leaves to form and grow).

School Standards

$\mathcal{T}eacher\ \mathcal{A}ctivity$: Mapping Your School Standards

Go to your school Website, if available, and find the relevant standards and include them in your folder.

EXAMPLE OF SCHOOL STANDARDS

Here is an example of what standards one suburban school has recommended for use in K–2 science.

1. **Kindergarten**
   - Examine the characteristics of living things.
   - Explore various kinds of movement affected by pushes and pulls.
   - Identify properties of gravity.
   - Describe and identify various objects in the daytime and night sky.

2. **Grade 1**
   - Differentiate between plants and animals.
   - Classify plants and animals to distinguish features.
   - Identify the properties of a magnetic force.
   - Classify objects based on magnetic properties.
   - Describe the interactions between the earth's soil, rocks, and water.
   - Identify how water flows.

3. **Grade 2**
   - Differentiate the needs of living and nonliving things.
   - Identify plant and animal adaptations to various habitats.
   - Investigate the basic qualities of light and light sources.
   - Produce and identify the colors of the spectrum.
   - Describe and identify how forces affect motion and how motion is measured.
   - Demonstrate an understanding of sound waves, pitch, and volume.
   - Classify dinosaurs by their characteristics.
   - Investigate fossils.
   - Observe weather changes.
   - Observe changes in the day and night sky.

You have collected a large folder containing the national, state, district, and school standards; examples of activities; and addresses for numerous Websites where you can find additional activities. With these in hand, you can begin to assess your readiness to teach science in your classroom. After completing the activities in the previous chapters, do you now feel more knowledgeable about what needs to be taught in your science classroom?

Classroom Standards

In your classroom, you make final decisions as to what science will be taught and how it will be taught. You are somewhat in control of what curriculum is enacted in your classroom; your teaching is always framed by who you are. So far you have collected all the standards. Now what? How do you convert all this information to your classroom teaching? How do you foster relationships with other teachers, mentors, administrators, parents, and community members to enhance your science teaching? You now have to work on creating a science curriculum for your day-to-day teaching that is standards compliant and relevant to your children's personal context.

Teacher Activity: Science Lessons

Explore your state, district, or city Websites for science lessons and activities. Collect these in your folder.

How Do You Plan to Be an Effective Science Teacher?

This question is probably the most open-ended of the four questions. Children have ideas about the natural world; your task is to discover and identify these ideas. Your destination has been determined by the national *Standards* and *Benchmarks*. Even though the answer to the question "How do I get there?" might be provided in curricular materials, you will still need to consider the appropriateness of the suggested sequence of procedures, the proposed modes of instruction, the organization of children, and the selection and management of materials. You still need to plan for what happens in your classroom on a day-to-day basis.

Developing Your Plan

Consider the following guidelines, which are partially informed by the U.S. DoE (1991).

1. What works best for young children

   - Children, especially younger ones, learn science best and understand scientific ideas better if they are able to investigate and experiment.

   - Hands-on science can also help children think critically and gain confidence in their own ability to solve problems.

   - What engages very young children? Things they can see, touch, manipulate, modify; situations that allow them to figure out what happens; events and puzzles they can investigate—in short, the very stuff of science.

   - Hands-on science can be messy and time consuming. Before you get started, see what is involved in an activity, including how long it will take.

   - Less is more. The best way to help children learn to think scientifically is to introduce them to just a few topics in depth.

2. Finding the right activity for your class

   - Different children have different interests and need different science projects. A sand-and-rock collection that was a big hit with a six-year-old girl may not be a big hit with her six-year-old twin brother.

   - Knowing your children is the best way to find suitable activities. Encourage activities that are neither too hard nor too easy. If in doubt, err on the easy side, since something too difficult may give the idea that science itself is too hard.

   - Age suggestions on book jackets or games are just that—suggestions. They may not reflect the interest or ability of the child. A child who is interested in a subject can often handle material for a higher age group, while a child who is not interested in or has not been exposed to the subject may need to start with something for a younger age group.

   - Consider a child's personality and social habits. Some projects are best done alone, others in a group; some require help, others require little or no supervision. Solitary activities may bore some, while group projects may frighten others.

   - Select activities appropriate for the child's environment. A brightly lighted city is not the best place for star gazing; you might consider a trip to a planetarium. If you are in a suburban or rural area, you can consider star-gazing activities with family involvement, maybe linked to a family science night.

   - Allow your children to help select the activities. If you don't know whether Phoebe would rather collect dinosaurs or grow beans, ask her.

When she picks something she wants to do, she will learn more and have a better time doing it.

3. Helping children emerge as scientists

- The early years of elementary school are a good time to start teaching children scientific ethics. You should tell them how important it is to be accurate about their observations.

- Children need to know it is all right to make mistakes: we all make mistakes, and we can learn from them. Explain that important discoveries are made only if we are willing and able to correct our mistakes.

- Help your children understand that we cannot always take someone else's word; it is important to find out for ourselves.

Rationale for Teaching a Topic

Why should your children be expected to demonstrate the desired behavior in your lesson or activity? As children progress through school and through their science classes one of the most frequently asked questions is "Why do I have to study this?" You must know why you are teaching and what you are teaching and clearly communicate this to your children. For example, you are teaching safety procedures during a field trip because you are taking your class to visit the zoo, and each child needs to know how to be safe while at the zoo. Or your children are learning about the parts of a seed because next week they will begin a class project on "Growing Your Own Salad."

Teacher Activity: Setting Goals for Teaching a Lesson?

Answer these questions as you do your lesson planning:

- What am I hoping my children will get out of this science experience?

- What science concepts do I want to help them develop?

- What should my children be able to do as a result of their interactions in this science experience?

- What materials and procedures will be most conducive to the desired behaviors?

- How will I engage my children in the experience?

- What will my children learn from this experience?

- What degree of mastery of learning should my children demonstrate?

If you use the questions in the activity as a guide as you plan for instruction, they can serve as the compass, or global positioning system (GPS), for your journey, always keeping you on the right path.

As you plan your route, here are some things to consider:

- Where are your children in relation to the goals of the lesson?
- Given the physical constraints of the classroom and the presence or absence of equipment, can the children achieve the goal?
- Which of the children's entry behaviors and existing understandings (and misunderstandings) specifically relate to the goal?
- What individual differences exist among the children in terms of their abilities to achieve the goal?
- What similarities are there?

Once you develop a better understanding of where the children are in relation to the goals, you can more accurately predict the amount of time they'll need to achieve it.

As you specify what you expect children to do, remember to use terms that can be readily observed. This will help you better recognize the behavior and know that your children are performing adequately. In K–2 science, some of these terms can include: *arrange, classify, compare, construct, list, measure, organize,* and *select.* These terms are extremely important and become the pivotal component of your instruction. They help you to answer the question "What should my children be able to do as a result of interacting with the materials I have provided?"

Deciding on Your Mode of Science Instruction

This is probably the most exciting part of planning. This is where you can demonstrate your creativity and imagination. You have limitless resources from which to select. Here are some possibilities in the K–2 classroom:

- hands-on inquiry
- involvement of children in investigating materials then talking about what they have discovered
- technology-based lessons involving heavy emphasis on computers, probes, smart boards, Websites, etc.
- project-based learning
- readings by the teacher, the children, or both
- short lecture by the teacher, or lecture combined with materials and demonstration
- science corners for self-directed learning

- science "show and tell" by the children
- games or simulation activities
- field trips—away from, near, or on the school grounds
- pantomimes, plays, and other dramatizations
- scientists in the classroom
- interviews

These are just a few of the possibilities. Your selection of any one mode or a combination of several depends on your instructional objective for the children and the type of technology to which you have access. Which instructional mode will best help your children achieve the intended goal? Remember that the repeated use of one mode of instruction over a long period of time can eventually lose its appeal. You need variety to spice up your science class and to maintain the interest of your children.

Organizing Your Class

You also need to consider lessons designed for the total class, for small groups, or for individuals. Class size can range from under ten children to over thirty-five. If you are in a school system in which small classes exist, your instructional modes will be very different from systems in which the class size is over thirty. Using small groups can provide children with opportunities for sharing, discussing and cooperative learning.

As young children engage in small groups, they develop skills of self-control and self-discipline, which are necessary social skills. Small groups can also provide the opportunity for young children to have an active, personal, and direct involvement in their own learning process; to express their creativity; and to begin to realize that they can learn independently of their teacher. There are many advantages to small group work, but it is also very difficult to arrange successfully. Do not be discouraged if it does not work the first time around. Keep persisting, since the advantages outweigh the disadvantages.

Selecting and Managing Materials

Effective science encounters for children involve their interacting with materials—more specifically, with real objects from the natural world. Whenever possible, use real objects in your science classroom. Selecting what you hope will be the most meaningful learning materials for your children is a crucial task. You can complete all the mental preparations for presenting a meaningful science encounter and then see your efforts fizzle because the materials you selected were meaningless or mishandled.

Here are some issues that the U.S. DoE has suggested that you consider as you select learning materials for your class:

1. **Safety.** Avoid objects that might be harmful to the children. Be prepared for breaks, spills, and stains. If objects are to be tasted or smelled, first check the children's records for information on allergies or other susceptibilities. Get parental permission before allowing children to taste material. Small animals such as gerbils, hamsters, or crayfish should be handled cautiously.

2. **Materials.** Balances should balance; microscopes should magnify; support stands should support; magnets should attract magnetic materials; wheels on axles should turn. Test materials before use in the classroom; if they do not work, then change your activity. Also, try to have a sufficient quantity of materials so that not many children will have to wait their turn. Very young children generally cannot handle relatively small or large objects easily. Most young children are not hesitant to use materials, but a few may shy away from objects that look very fragile or overly complicated.

3. **Distribution of materials.** Develop any workable technique that will let you distribute the materials to the class easily and quickly. Much valuable time can be wasted if materials are distributed carelessly. You might try packaging the items, or arranging supply centers in various sections of the room, or appointing certain children as helpers.

4. **Timing.** As you arrange and manage your materials you need to consider timing. When should the children actually have the materials in their hands or before their eyes? Should they have them at the very beginning of the lesson? Generally, children are more interested in interacting with materials than with spoken or printed word. So if it is important that something be said or read first, do not distribute the materials until this is done. This strategy also allows the children to give their undivided attention to the materials when they are distributed.

5. **Location of use.** Decide in advance where the children are to use the materials, and anticipate the consequences. Prepare for the inevitable; children tend to become more excited or even unruly when interacting with materials on a floor area or outdoors than when seated at desks or around tables.

6. **Need for familiarity time with materials before activity.** Remember that children need some initial time to investigate and handle the materials freely (within the limits of safety, of course) and independently. In some cases, this might be the first time your children are seeing this material.

Give them some time to become familiar with the material. If you rush into your planned procedures too quickly, you might stifle some potential learning. Often their first interaction with the materials will produce the questions that can guide the inquiry in your classroom.

7. **Establishing rules.** Try to anticipate any misuse of materials and the effects of overstimulation. If the children have had very few opportunities to interact with science materials in a classroom, their excitement over even seemingly mundane objects can be astonishing. It might be necessary to establish some behavioral guidelines before the materials are distributed.

8. **Clean-up procedure.** Develop and maintain thorough cleanup procedures. You'll be doing yourself an enormous favor and also helping the children develop a worthwhile habit. You might assign a rotating cleanup detail until the children voluntarily assume the responsibility. Label your storage containers so that the objects can be easily identified and inventoried.

9. **Sharing materials with other teachers.** If you have to share your materials with other teachers, work together to establish clear rules to ensure that materials are always returned to their designated places and replaced if necessary.

Curriculum Development

Teacher Activity: **Focus Questions**

In planning, consider the following questions:

How do I begin to plan my schedule?

_____

_____

How can I use standards to create a compliant curriculum?

_____

_____

An important aspect of the question: "How do I get there?" involves looking at what other teachers have done as they plan their journeys.

Ideas from Other Science Teachers

EXAMPLE OF A K–2 SCHEDULE FOR AN URBAN SCHOOL

Kindergarten

1. Seasons

   - Observe the weather elements—temperature, precipitation, clouds, wind.

   - Observe a particular tree from early fall until early summer.

2. Plants and Animals

   - Study plants growing in the neighborhood, perhaps near the playground or a nearby park.

   - Plant their own garden—in the community, on the school grounds, or even in window boxes—to observe the way plants grow and change.

First Grade

1. Weather and Season

   - Keep a journal of seasonal weather changes as they experience them.

   - Keep track of precipitation levels by setting up a tool for collecting the precipitation and measuring it daily. Using this information, children can use this information to hypothesize about what happens during certain seasons and months.

   - Keep a cloud journal, with space to draw what they observe. In doing this, children will familiarize themselves with the characteristics that different types of clouds have.

2. Animal Diversity

   - Observe and learn about whatever wildlife is common in the neighborhood, such as pigeons, English sparrows, and/or squirrels. Learn about their anatomy, what they eat, and how they survive in the city.

   - See if you can find a pigeon raiser who would be willing to have your class visit his coop (not uncommon in the city). Visit, observe, and hypothesize about what will happen as the egg hatches and develops into a bird. Children could also use this to acknowledge that animals closely resemble their parents.

3. Plant Diversity

- Seek out plants or flowers growing close by or in the school yard. From this, look at the different parts of a plant by dissecting one as a class. (Need to get permission.)

- Take a nature walk in order to discover how plants differ, even in the school neighborhood.

Second Grade

1. Properties of Water

- Explore the physical properties of water by studying water (rain, lakes and rivers, ocean) around the school in the fall, winter, and spring.

- Observe rain puddles and observe which substances they notice mixing with water and which ones they don't (car oil).

2. Earth Materials

- Look for signs of weathering on the surrounding buildings.

- Go on a rock hunt and point out all the different types of rock in their neighborhood. Children could later research about the types of rocks they found. This can also be done with buildings, if any old, fancy ones exist near your school. Hunt for different types of marble, granite, etc.

- Compare and sort found rocks by color, texture, patterns, size, hardness, and softness.

- Study soil samples from various neighborhood locations; analyze for compaction, components, nutrients, and pollutants. Analyze plant growth from each location.

3. Habitat Study

- Study the habitats of pigeons, squirrels, rats, mice, cockroaches in and around the school.

4. Animals and Plants in Their Environment

- Adopt a tree to study the seasonal changes.

- Observe different plants' life cycles; compare and contrast plants at different points in their life cycles.

- Observe and keep a journal on a specific species such as pigeons; record observations, questions, hypotheses.

Source: Example originated by Lindsay McPherson and Andrea Elias

Teacher Activity: Developing Your Own Curriculum

Here are some questions used by my colleague, Jason Blaustein, to think about as develop your own curriculum.

Phase 1. Selecting and setting up your lesson

- What are your goals for the lesson?
- What is it you want your children to know and understand about science as a result of the lesson?
- How will you build on your children's previous knowledge?
- What concepts and ideas do your children need to know in order to begin the task?
- What questions will you ask to help your children access their prior knowledge?
- What misconceptions might your children have?
- What are your expectations for your children?
- What resources will your children have to use?
- Will children work independently, in pairs, or in small groups?
- How will you arrange the class?

Phase 2. Supporting children as they engage in the lesson

- How will you introduce the lesson?
- What questions will you ask to focus their thinking?
- What questions will you ask to assess your children understanding of concepts?
- How will you encourage your children to share their thinking with their peers?
- How will you ensure that all your children remain engaged?
- What will you do if some children finish the activity and become bored or disruptive?

Phase 3. Sharing and discussing the activity

- How will you frame the class discussion so that you accomplish your goals?
- What specific questions will you ask so that your children will make sense of the scientific concepts you are teaching?
- What will you do in the following classes that will build on this lesson?

Refer to the list of topics you generated in the Teacher Activity: Your State Standards and Teaching Topics and brainstorm strategies for teaching those topics. The lessons on the following pages provide examples you can use in setting up your own curriculum plan.

Dr. Robert Wallace planned the following investigations around student questions. His teaching philosophy is based on the belief that science studies in elementary school should have the following characteristics:

- The questions asked should be drawn from problems that concern children and adults.

- Although the questions are of an adult nature, it is possible to investigate them at an appropriate elementary school level.

- The questions should not have an obvious answer, but children should have enough experience with the phenomena to make reasonable predictions.

- The questions can be answered by collecting and examining data rather than by seeking opinions, consensus, majority vote, etc.

- Although the teacher may not know the answers to the questions, the teacher is essential to the process of investigation.

- It is important to keep all of the data collected so that the work can be reinvestigated if necessary.

- While some conclusions may be made, most of the investigations should raise more questions.

- At no time is it possible for anyone to know if they have found the "right" or "true" answer.

- All answers are framed in terms of new ideas to be tested. The conclusions may be complex, so any predictions based on them must indicate the degree of confidence in the result.

- When the work is finished, it is shared so that it becomes part of the body of knowledge that has been learned.

LESSON EXAMPLE 1: Are the Leaves Beneath a Tree the Same Shape as the Leaves Growing on the Tree?

As part of a year-long tree study, students were studying leaf shapes from trees in a nearby park. As they played with the leaves, some students wondered how whether leaves that fall from trees stay close to the tree or travel farther away from the tree. This question led to the following leaf investigation:

The students chose an area in the park that was relatively undisturbed by human traffic and park activities. The site selected was beneath a tree that had oval leaves, probably a beech tree based on later identification but labeled an "oval-leafed" tree by the students.

We collected a plastic bag of leaf litter from beneath the tree and took it back to the classroom. There the leaves were organized according to shape and counted. If they could be identified then they were, otherwise they were given descriptive names. The results were plotted on graph paper and column graphs were created. Figure 8.2 shows an example of one of these graphs, plotted using a spreadsheet program.

We discovered that in this case, there were many leaves that apparently came from the nearby tree. However, there were also many leaves from other trees in the park. In addition, there was a considerable amount of broken-up leaf litter that could not be identified as to which tree it came from. The students also noted that there were no needle-shaped leaves, even though there are trees with needle-shaped leaves in the vicinity. This suggested to the students that needle-shaped leaves do not travel far from their source while leaves from broad-leaved trees may.

Figure 8.2 Results of Leaf Investigation

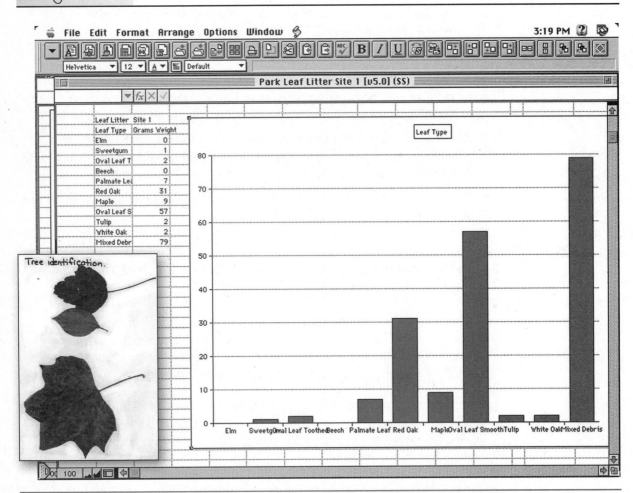

LESSON EXAMPLE 2: How Much Liquid Water Is in Ice and Snow?

After a significant snow storm, students wondered how much liquid water there was in snow and ice. We set up the following investigation:

In one of three plastic containers (see the photo), students gently loaded it with newly fallen snow. In the second container, they packed it with as much snow as possible without going over the top. In the third, they filled it as much as possible with broken pieces of ice.

They then let the three containers melt and the students measured the height of the water in each container.

They discovered that all containers had significantly less water than any of the solid versions of water that were studied. The one with the most water was the one where the students had packed the ice into the container. The one with packed snow was next. Finally, the one with newly fallen snow had the least amount of water when it melted.

The students were surprised to see that snow and ice contained significantly less water than they expected. This suggested to them that the reason had something to do with the amount of air that was trapped in the ice and snow.

LESSON EXAMPLE 3: How Many Minibeasts Are in the Soil in the Park?

While studying soil, the students wondered whether there were many organisms that lived in the soil in the park. We decided to find out.

Using an invertebrate identification chart, students placed a scoop of soil on the chart and identified the minibeasts that they could see. In this investigation, we did not find many minibeasts except for earthworms. Students measured the length of the earthworms and graphed them as shown in Figure 8.3.

They discovered that the graph of the sizes of the worms indicated that smaller worms were more numerous than larger worms. If the length of the worm is proportional to its age then there are more young worms in the park soil than older worms.

Figure 8.3   Results of Minibeast Investigation

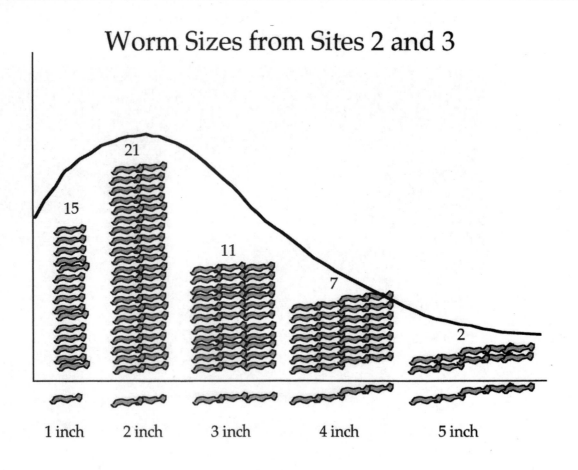

Worm Sizes from Sites 2 and 3

LESSON EXAMPLE 4: What Are Some of the Microscopic Organisms That Live in Fresh Water?

The park near the school has a small fresh-water pond that has many fish in it. The students wondered about what the fish ate. They decided that they wanted to look at pond water under the microscope to see if there were any creatures visible there. We collected some pond water and looked at it under the microscope. Using the identification chart of common pond invertebrates, they tried to identify any visible creatures.

In order to count the number of creatures, each student had a microscope with a drop of water on a slide. If a child saw an organism, she would raise her hand, and the teacher would confirm the identification. If other children saw the same organism, we would record the number of children who saw that particular creature. Using this technique, we were able to produce the graph in Figure 8.4.

The main organisms in the water studied were ostracods, aquatic worms and insect larvae. Using this approach, it was possible for first- and second-graders to make a quantitative estimate of the numbers of some of the microorganisms that could be found in the pond. They were also able to make fairly detailed drawings of some of the organisms that they could see (Figure 8.5).

Figure 8.4   **Results of Fresh-Water Creatures Study**

Creatures from the Meer (site F, near beach)

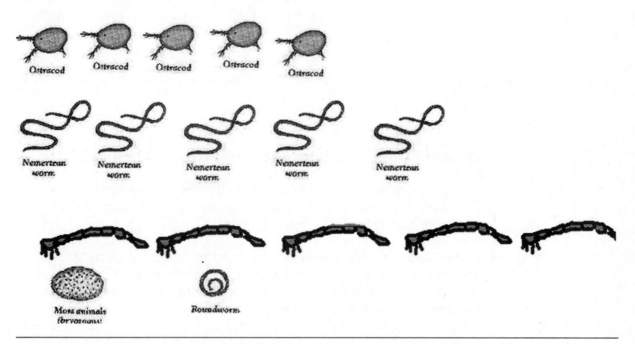

Figure 8.5 Water Flea

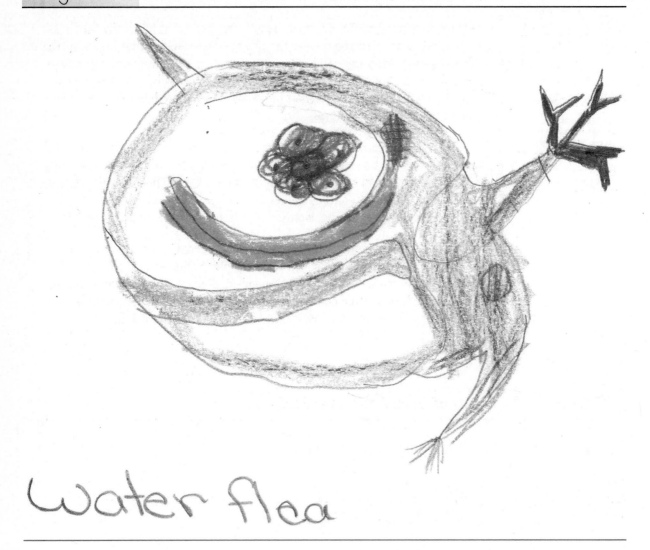

water flea

LESSON EXAMPLE 5: What Organisms Live in a Rotting Log?

An important topic in the study of nature in early elementary school is habitat. In the park we were looking for habitats of various organisms, such as birds, when some students noticed a rotting log (see the photo).

This was an opportunity to look more closely at the log to see if we could discover why it was decaying. The students carefully opened up the log and made drawings of what they saw. It was possible to see that a decaying log was comprised of a larger number of organisms.

How Will You Know When You Have Arrived at Your Best Level of Practice?

There is no definite answer to this question. You never really arrive. You are always trying to be an effective science teacher and so you are always changing. Your children are constantly changing, and the body of scientific knowledge is constantly changing. The state and national tests will tell you how your children are performing, but you want to do more than have your children perform well on standardized tests. You want them to be emerging scientists on their way to becoming scientifically literate. Tests are important, but it is important to look at additional feedback on your success in teaching science, which enables your children to emerge as scientists. The most appropriate way to answer this question is to closely examine what is happening to you and what is happening to your children as a result of their exposure to science.

At the end of each science class, reflect on the following questions:

- What went well today?
- How successful was my class?
- Why was it a success?

- What did not go well today?
- Where did I go wrong?
- What changes should I make in my class tomorrow?
- If I could repeat this lesson, what would I do differently?

By continuing to reflect on these questions after each class session, you will eventually discover your strengths and weaknesses. Use these reflections for honest self-confrontation and accurate self-evaluation and to plan for your day-to-day science teaching

You will know that your children are being provided with adequate opportunities for learning science, according to the science professional development community and the U.S. DoE, if they are

- handling materials, living and nonliving, without fear
- designing, making, or manipulating apparatus using a variety of materials, including state-of-the-art technology and readily available items
- moving around freely and finding the materials they need
- discussing their work with each other or with you and classroom visitors
- busy doing things they feel are important
- trying to work out for themselves what to do from step to step
- not expecting to be told what to do
- puzzling over a problem
- comparing their ideas or observations with those of others

You will know that you have created a situation in which science can be learned if your children

- have a clear idea of what they want to find out, investigate or observe
- take the initiative in suggesting what to do and how to set about it
- try out ideas "to see what happens"
- observe things closely by watching, listening, touching, smelling
- try different ways of approaching a problem
- classify things according to their properties or characteristics
- make some record of what they find out or observe
- use instruments for aiding observation or measurement
- devise and apply tests to find out what things will do
- make predictions of what they expect to find or to happen

- look for evidence to support the statements they make
- try to quantify their observations
- confirm their findings carefully before accepting them as evidence

If you are a success at teaching science, visitors to your classroom and school should easily be able to find answers to the following questions that you should also consider as you plan for teaching science. The answers will help you determine if you have arrived and will let visitors determine if real science is happening in your classroom/school.

Classroom

- Do you see displays related to science? Science learning centers?
- Are science-related drawings on the bulletin boards? Are there plants, terrariums, aquariums, or collections (of rocks or insects, etc.)?
- Do you see any science equipment in evidence? Are there magnifiers? Magnets? Pictures? Computers?
- In science classes, do children work with materials, or is the teacher always reading or demonstrating?
- Do children discuss their ideas, predictions, and explanations with each other as well as with the teacher?
- What facilities and resources are available to teach science?
- How often is science taught? Every day, once a week, or only once in a while?
- Does the teacher have clear goals and objectives for teaching science?
- How often is science taught? Every day, once a week, or infrequently?
- Are children given opportunities to do hands-on science projects?
- Are children taken on field trips?
- Do teachers welcome assistance from parents and community members?
- Are activities available for parents to use at home to supplement what is done at school?

School

- Does the school library contain science books? If so, are children encouraged to read them?
- Is there enough space in the classrooms or elsewhere in the school for children to conduct experiments?

- If the school budget for science is inadequate, has the teacher tried to obtain resources from private or public funding sources?
- Is there a family science night?

So now you are ready to lead your K–2 children on a journey of exploration into the world of science. You have been preparing for your journey of teaching emerging scientists. You have collected all your gear—content, pedagogical strategies, standards, materials, and information on your fellow travelers. And now it is time to begin the journey.

Take-Away Thought

An effective science teacher has a well-structured but flexible plan. Time to walk the talk. Enjoy the journey.

Appendix 1

The National Science Education Standards and Benchmarks for Science Literacy

What Are the Standards for Grades K–4 Science Content?

In 1989, the National Governors Association endorsed national education goals and set the stage for the development of national education standards. The mathematics standards developed by the National Council of Teachers of Mathematics (NCTM) were the first national standards to appear. In 1991, the National Research Council (NRC) began the development of the *National Science Education Standards (NSES),* with support from the Department of Education and the National Science Foundation. In 1996, after input from numerous scientists, science educators, teachers and other citizens, the final version was published. The objective of the *National Science Education Standards* is to help achieve scientific literacy for all members of our society.

The NRC defines scientific literacy as the knowledge and understanding of scientific concepts and processes required for personal decision making, participation in civic and cultural affairs, and economic productivity. It also includes specific types of abilities.

The *National Science Education Standards* identify

- what it means to be a scientifically literate citizen
- what should be taught at various grades levels
- what knowledge and skills teachers should have
- how children should be assessed
- how school districts should implement curriculum changes that will result in greater scientific literacy

The *National Science Education Standards* (National Research Council, 1996, p. 22) include:

- **Standards for science teaching.** The science teaching standards describe what teachers of science at all grade levels should know and be able to do.
- **Standards for professional development for teachers of science.** The professional development standards present a vision for the development of professional knowledge and skill among teachers (http://www.nap.edu/ readingroom/books/nses/4.html).
- **Standards for assessment in science education.** The assessment standards provide criteria against which to judge the quality of assessment practices.
- **Standards for science content.** The science content standards outline what children should know, understand, and be able to do in the natural sciences over the course of K–12 education.
- **Standards for science education programs.** The science education program standards describe the conditions necessary for quality school science programs.
- **Standards for science education systems.** The science education system standards consist of criteria for judging the performance of the overall science education system.

The *National Science Education Standards* are standards for all Americans. Equity is an underlying principle of the *Standards* and should pervade all aspects of science education. They apply to all children, regardless of age, gender, cultural or ethnic background, disabilities, aspirations, or interest and motivation in science. Different children will achieve understanding in different ways, and different children will achieve different degrees of depth and breadth of understanding depending on interest, ability, and context. But all children can develop the knowledge and skills described in the *Standards,* even as some children go well beyond these levels.

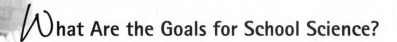

What Are the Goals for School Science?

The goals for school science that underlie the *National Science Education Standards* are to educate children who are able to

- experience the richness and excitement of knowing about and understanding the natural world
- use appropriate scientific processes and principles in making personal decisions
- engage intelligently in public discourse and debate about matters of scientific and technological concern
- increase their economic productivity through the use of the knowledge, understanding, and skills developed in their science education

This section focuses only on the standards for science content. You should, however, become familiar with standards for the other areas. The content standards—organized by K–4, 5–8, and 9–12 grade levels—provide expectations for the development of student understanding and ability over the course of K–12 education. Content is defined to include

- inquiry
- the traditional subject areas of physical, life, and earth and space sciences
- connections between science and technology
- science in personal and social perspectives
- the history and nature of science

The content standards are supplemented with information on developing student understanding, and they include fundamental concepts that underlie each standard.

Teacher Activity: Mapping the National Standards

Create an online folder or a hard copy in a folder or binder. As you complete the activities below, either store in your folder or print out the relevant standards and create your own current reference guide. This will be invaluable as you begin developing your class' curriculum.

1. Locate the national standards: http://www.nap.edu/readingroom/books/nses/overview. html#organization or http://www.nap.edu/readingroom/books/nses.

2. Find the standards for grades K–4, then print and file them.

What Are the Standards for Grades K–4 Science Content?

Let us take a look at the standards for K–4 science content. The list on the following pages is a summary of the requirements of each content standard, as provided by the *National Science Education Standards*.

- *Content standard A* asks children in grades K–4 to develop abilities necessary to do scientific inquiry and understand scientific inquiry. In the early years of school, children investigate earth materials, organisms, and properties of common objects, developing vocabulary and inquiry skills. The national standards focus on the process of doing investigations and of children developing the ability to ask scientific questions, investigate aspects of the world around them, and use these observations to construct reasonable explanations for posed questions. Children ask questions about objects, organisms, and events in the environment. Children plan and conduct simple investigations, employing simple equipment and tools to gather data and extend the senses in order to construct explanations.

- *Content standard B* requires that children develop an understanding of the properties of objects and materials, the position and motion of objects, and the concepts of light, heat, electricity, and magnetism. Children are expected to compare, describe, and sort as they begin to form explanations of the world relying on their experiences and teacher-provided opportunities to grow in those understandings. Physical science in grades K–4 includes topics that give children a chance to increase their understanding of the characteristics of objects and materials they encounter daily.

- *Content standard C* requires that children develop an understanding of the characteristics of organisms, the life cycles of organisms, and organisms within their environment. During the elementary years, children are building their understanding of biological concepts through direct experiences with living things, their life cycles and their habitats. These experiences are organically derived through a sense of wonder and questions. Making sense of the way organisms live in their environments helps to develop understanding of the diversity of life and how all living organisms depend on the living and nonliving environment for survival.

- *Content standard D* requires that children develop an understanding of the properties of earth materials, objects in the sky, and changes in the earth and sky. Children in K–4 are encouraged to observe closely the objects and materials in their environment, note their properties, distinguish one from another, and develop their own understanding and explanations of how things have come to be the way they are. As the children become more familiar with the world around them, they are guided to observe changes, including cyclical changes (such as day and night), predictable trends (such as growth and decay), and less consistent changes (such as weather or the appearance of meteors).

- *Content standard E* requires that children develop an understanding of the abilities of technological design, an understanding about science and technology, and the ability to distinguish between natural objects and objects made by humans. The science and technology standard is designed to connect children to the designed world, offer them experience in making models of useful things, and introduce them to laws of nature through their understandings of how technological objects and systems work.

- *Content standard F* requires that children develop an understanding of personal health, characteristics and changes in populations, types of resources, changes in environments, and science and technology in local challenges. The central ideas relating to the standard focus on the development of children's awareness of their actions as citizens.

- *Content standard G* requires that children develop an understanding of science as a human endeavor. Teachers are asked to build on children's natural tendency to ask questions and investigate their world. By learning about scientific inquiry and the people who helped shape science, children are given the scaffolding to develop sophisticated ideas related to the history and nature of science, which will be developed throughout their science education.

The content standards do not dictate a national curriculum; however, they emphasize that the science experiences for grades K–12 need to be broad based. Each school and district must translate the *National Science Education Standards* into a program that reflects local contexts and policies. The program standards discuss the planning and actions needed to provide comprehensive and coordinated experiences for all children across all grade levels. The *Standards,* however, do not dictate the order, organization, or framework for science programs. Each state has the leeway to decide how programs will be enacted

The instruction, program, and assessment that are emphasized by the *NSES* all promote the notion of inquiry in science teaching. What does inquiry mean in the context of science teaching? According to the *Standards,* inquiry into authentic questions generated from student experiences is the central strategy for teaching science. The *Standards* encourage teachers to focus on inquiry as it relates to the real-life experiences of children and to guide children to fashion their own investigations. Much of the current research in science education seeks to define what inquiry is, how it is enacted in the classroom, and how teachers can develop and implement inquiry-based experiences in their classrooms. As you begin to plan your science experiences for grades K–2 children, you will realize that the term *inquiry* is used to describe a wide array of teaching strategies, including discovery learning, learning-cycle-structured activities, open inquiry, and project-based learning. In general, the more direct experiences children have with materials, the greater the opportunity for them to ask and answer their own questions, thus leading to a deeper and more profound construction of their own understanding.

Teacher Activity: Standards Table

As you begin to plan for teaching, complete Table A1.1. The standard is listed in column 1; the content understanding that your K–4 students need to develop in column 2. In column 3, you can list the inquiry and process skills that have been mentioned in association with this standard. Next, begin looking for Websites, textbooks, journals (e.g., *Science and Children*, an NSTA publication) for activities that you can use as you begin to plan for teaching and list these in column 4.

Table A1.1 Standards for K–4 Science Content

Standard	Content	Inquiry/Process Skills	Web/Text Reference for Activity
A	All students should develop • abilities necessary to do scientific inquiry • understanding about scientific inquiry		
B	All students should develop an understanding of • properties of objects and materials • position and motion of objects • light, heat, electricity, and magnetism		

(continued on next page)

Table A1.1 Standards for K–4 Science Content (continued)

Standard	Content	Inquiry/Process Skills	Web/Text Reference for Activity
C	All students should develop understanding of • characteristics of organisms • life cycles of organisms • organisms and environments		
D	All students should develop an understanding of • properties of earth materials • objects in the sky • changes in earth and sky		
E	All students should develop • abilities of technological design • understanding about science and technology • abilities to distinguish between natural objects and objects made by humans		
F	All students should develop understanding of • personal health • characteristics and changes in populations • types of resources • changes in environments • science and technology in local challenges		
G	All students should develop understanding of • science as a human endeavor		

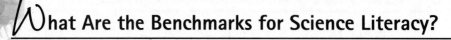

What Are the Benchmarks for Science Literacy?

The *Benchmarks for Science Literacy,* developed by Project 2061, specify how children should progress toward science literacy and recommend what they should know and be able to do by the time they reach certain grade levels. Project 2061's *Benchmarks* are statements of what all children should know or be able to do in science, mathematics, and technology by the end of grades 2, 5, 8, and 12.

Teacher Activity: Using the *Benchmarks*

Table A1.2 lists the *Benchmarks* in columns 1 and 2. Fill in where the *Benchmark* is covered in your curriculum in column 3.

Table A1.2 *Benchmarks for Science Literacy for K–2*

The Nature of Science

Topic	What children should know by the end of second grade	Where this is covered in my curriculum
The Scientific World View	1. When a science investigation is done the way it was done before, we expect to get a very similar result. 2. Science investigations generally work the same way in different places.	
Scientific Inquiry	1. People can often learn about things around them by just observing those things carefully, but sometimes they can learn more by doing something to the things and noting what happens. 2. Tools such as thermometers, magnifiers, rulers, or balances often give more information about things than can be obtained by just observing things without their help. 3. Describing things as accurately as possible is important in science because it enables people to compare their observations with those of others. 4. When people give different descriptions of the same thing, it is usually a good idea to make some fresh observations instead of just arguing about who is right.	
The Scientific Enterprise	1. Everybody can do science and invent things and ideas. 2. In doing science, it is often helpful to work with a team and to share findings with others. All team members should reach their own individual conclusions, however, about what the findings mean. 3. A lot can be learned about plants and animals by observing them closely, but care must be taken to know the needs of living things and how to provide for them in the classroom.	

Table A1.2 *Benchmarks for Science Literacy* for K–2

The Nature of Technology

Topic	What children should know by the end of second grade	Where this is covered in my curriculum
Technology and Science	1. Tools are used to do things better or more easily and to do some things that could not otherwise be done at all. In technology, tools are used to observe, measure, and make things. 2. When trying to build something or to get something to work better, it usually helps to follow directions if there are any or to ask someone who has done it before for suggestions.	
Design and Systems	People may not be able to actually make or do everything that they can design.	
Issues in Technology	1. People, alone or in groups, are always inventing new ways to solve problems and get work done. The tools and ways of doing things that people have invented affect all aspects of life. 2. When a group of people wants to build something or try something new, they should try to figure out ahead of time how it might affect other people.	

Table A1.2 *Benchmarks for Science Literacy* for K–2

The Physical Setting

Topic	What children should know by the end of second grade	Where this is covered in my curriculum
The Universe	1. There are more stars in the sky than anyone can easily count, but they are not scattered evenly, and they are not all the same in brightness or color. 2. The sun can be seen only in the daytime, but the moon can be seen sometimes at night and sometimes during the day. The sun, moon, and stars all appear to move slowly across the sky because of earth rotation. 3. The moon looks a little different every day, but it looks the same again about every four weeks.	
The Earth	1. Some events in nature have a repeating pattern. The weather changes some from day to day, but things such as temperature and rain (or snow) tend to be high, low, or medium in the same months every year. 2. Water can be a liquid or a solid and can go back and forth from one form to the other. If water is turned into ice and then the ice is allowed to melt, the amount of water is the same as it was before freezing. 3. Water left in an open container disappears, but water in a closed container does not disappear.	
Processes that Shape the Earth	1. Chunks of rocks come in many sizes and shapes, from boulders to grains of sand and even smaller. 2. Change is something that happens to many things. 3. Animals and plants sometimes cause changes in their surroundings.	

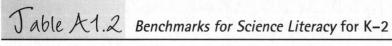 **Benchmarks for Science Literacy for K–2**

The Physical Setting (continued)

Topic	What children should know by the end of second grade	Where this is covered in my curriculum
The Structure of Matter	1. Objects can be described in terms of the materials they are made of (clay, cloth, paper, etc.) and their physical properties (color, size, shape, weight, texture, flexibility, etc.). 2. Things can be done to materials to change some of their properties, but not all materials respond the same way to what is done to them.	
Motion	1. Things move in many different ways, such as straight, zigzag, round and round, back and forth, and fast and slow. 2. The way to change how something is moving is to give it a push or a pull. 3. Things that make sound vibrate.	
Forces of Nature	1. Things near the Earth fall to the ground unless something holds them up. 2. Magnets can be used to make some things move without being touched.	

Table A1.2 *Benchmarks for Science Literacy* for K–2

The Living Environment

Topic	What children should know by the end of second grade	Where this is covered in my curriculum
Diversity of Life	1. Some animals and plants are alike in the way they look and in the things they do, and others are very different from one another. 2. Plants and animals have features that help them live in different environments. 3. Stories sometimes give plants and animals attributes they really do not have.	
Heredity	1. There is variation among individuals of one kind within a population. 2. Offspring are very much, but not exactly, like their parents and like one another.	
Cells	1. Magnifiers help people see things they could not see without them. 2. Most living things need water, food, and air.	
Interdependence of Life	1. Animals eat plants or other animals for food and may also use plants (or even other animals) for shelter and nesting. 2. Living things are found almost everywhere in the world. There are somewhat different kinds in different places.	
Flow of Matter and Energy	1. Plants and animals both need to take in water, and animals need to take in food. In addition, plants need light. 2. Many materials can be recycled and used again, sometimes in different forms.	

Table A1.2 *Benchmarks for Science Literacy* for K–2

	The Living Environment (continued)	
Topic	**What children should know by the end of second grade**	**Where this is covered in my curriculum**
Evolution of Life	1. Different plants and animals have external features that help them thrive in different kinds of places. 2. Some kinds of organisms that once lived on earth have completely disappeared, although they were something like others that are alive today.	

$\mathcal{T}$able A1.2 *Benchmarks for Science Literacy for K–2*

The Human Organism

Topic	What children should know by the end of second grade	Where this is covered in my curriculum
Human Identity	1. People have different external features, such as the size, shape, and color of hair, skin, and eyes, but they are more like one another than like other animals. 2. People need water, food, air, waste removal, and a particular range of temperatures in their environment, just as other animals do. 3. People tend to live in families and communities in which individuals have different roles.	
Human Development	1. All animals have offspring, usually with two parents involved. People may prevent some animals from producing offspring. 2. A human baby grows inside its mother until its birth. Even after birth, a human baby is unable to care for itself, and its survival depends on the care it receives from adults.	
Basic Functions and Learning	1. The human body has parts that help it seek, find, and take in food when it feels hunger: eyes and noses for detecting food; legs to get to it, arms to carry it away; and a mouth to eat it. 2. Senses can warn individuals about danger; muscles help them to fight, hide, or get out of danger. 3. The brain enables human beings to think and sends messages to other body parts to help them work properly.	

Table A1.2 *Benchmarks for Science Literacy* for K–2

The Human Organism (continued)

Topic	What children should know by the end of second grade	Where this is covered in my curriculum
Physical Health	1. Eating a variety of healthful foods and getting enough exercise and rest help people to stay healthy. 2. Some things people take into their bodies from the environment can hurt them. 3. Some diseases are caused by germs, some are not. Diseases caused by germs may be spread by people who have them. Washing one's hands with soap and water reduces the number of germs that can get into the body or that can be passed on to other people.	
Mental Health	1. People have many different feelings—sadness, joy, anger, fear, etc.—about events, themselves, and other people. 2. People react to personal problems in different ways. Some ways are more likely to be helpful than others. 3. Talking to someone (a friend, relative, teacher, or counselor) may help people understand their feelings and problems and what to do about them.	

Source: Modified from project2061.org/publications/bsl/online/bolintro.htm

Appendix 2

Science Content Information for Grades K–2

In teaching science, you begin with where your children are. Grade K–2 children bring a range of experiences into the classroom; they come to you with a wide range of "why" questions. How can you channel these experiences, their burning curiosity, and questions into meaningful and quality science education? In this Appendix, you are provided with some content you might need in order to begin developing your teaching plan for K–2 science.

As you examine the various state standards, the following content areas are covered most frequently:

- Kindergarten: Properties of objects, plants, animals, earth, weather, and water

- Grade 1: Properties of matter, weather and seasons, animal diversity

- Grade 2: Forces and motion, soil, plant diversity, life sciences

Kindergarten

Properties of Objects

In order to teach children about the properties of objects, teachers should know:

1. How to describe the physical properties of objects using the senses.

   - How to describe the shape of the object: Is the object round, irregular, octagonal, etc.?

   - How to describe the size of the object relative to another object: Is it bigger or smaller?

   - How to use instruments of measurement, such as rulers, to record and compare exact measurements.

   - How to describe the weight of an object: How heavy does it feel?

     ■ Speak about the object quantitatively: Is it heavier or lighter than another object?

     ■ Take measurements of the object using scales and balances.

   - How to describe the object in terms of color and luster.

   - How to describe the object in terms of flexibility and malleability.

2. How to describe the physical properties of objects (such as color, weight, shine and size) and to talk about the similarities and differences between objects.

3. How to introduce the use of science tools to help describe, observe, and group objects.

   - Objects can be described in terms of hot and cold.

     ■ Thermometers can act as a measurement tool.

   - Pan balances are used to record and compare the weights of objects.

   - Scientists can also use nonstandard units of measurement to describe objects.

     ■ Descriptive words such as *bigger* and *smaller* or *more* and *less* can be used to compare one object to another.

   - Hand lenses can be used to make observations of details of objects.

4. Objects can be described in terms of the materials they are made of.

   - Distinctions can be made between an object made of wood and one made of plastic or an object made of clay and one made of paper.

5. Objects can be grouped according to their properties and measurements.

   - For example, certain objects float and others sink and can be classified or grouped based on this property.

   - Certain objects have a particular texture or shine or shape, and similar objects can be grouped together based on these properties.

In California, the standards for Kindergarten require a deeper understanding of water and its properties. Teachers should understand that water can be a liquid, gas or a solid and can be made to change back and forth from one form to another through adding or removing heat energy. Kindergarteners are also required to have an understanding that water left in an open container evaporates into the air, changing state from a liquid to a gas, but that water kept in a closed container stays in the liquid form.

Plants

In order to teach the content of plants, teachers should know:

1. Organisms such as plants have basic needs in order to survive.

   - Plants need air, water, light, and suitable temperature in order to survive.

   - Living things, such as plants, grow and change when their basic needs are met.

     - Plants—when given water, proper soil conditions, and light—will change from a seedling into a plant.

2. Different structures enable each plant to live and thrive.

   - The roots, leaves, stems, flowers, and seeds of plants all contribute to the ability of the plant to survive.

     - The roots bring in nutrients and water.

     - The stem allows the plant to stand upright as well as containing the xylem and phloem, which deliver the water and nutrients throughout the plant.

     - The flower contains the sexual organs of the plant and the leaves absorb sunlight and exchange gases with the air.

3. Plants have adaptations that allow them to survive and thrive.

   - The leaves on certain trees fall in autumn and there is new plant growth in the spring as the weather warms and the ground thaws.

   - Some plants, such as maple trees and daffodils, go through cycles of growth in response to changes in their environment.

- Other plants, such as conifers, go through different cycles.

  - Special characteristics of these trees, such as their needles, allow them to survive during the winter.

4. How to make connections between the similarities and differences of certain plants.

   - How to make observations about the common characteristics of flowering plants and the common characteristics of trees with needles versus trees with leaves.

   - How to make observations and comparisons between perennial plants and seasonal plants.

A comparison can be made to the interdependence of the roots and the leaves to the wheel and axle of a car. (If one part is missing, the car will not work. The same thing is true for the plant. If the leaves are missing, the plant cannot absorb the sunlight. Conversely, if the roots are missing the plant cannot absorb its nutrients.)

California state standards also address the concept that stories can give plants and animals characteristics that they do not have, such as talking or walking.

Texas state standards identify the importance of children understanding that plants are made up of a network of interworking parts. All of the parts must be working in order for the plant to survive.

Animals

In order to teach the content of animals, teachers should know:

1. Animals have basic needs in order to survive and thrive as organisms.

   - Animals need air, water, food, and shelter.

2. Animals, like plants, are living things. As living things, animals grow, change and reproduce.

3. Animals have different structures that enable them to live and thrive.

   - Structures include wings for flying, fins for swimming, and legs for walking.

   - Animals have structures that are important for sensory input, including eyes for seeing, a nose for smelling, ears for hearing, a tongue for helping with food intake and skin; these function for protection from the environment as well as sensing touch.

   - Some animals also have defense mechanisms such as claws.

4. Living things, such as animals, have offspring that closely resemble their parents.

   - Dogs have puppies, cats have kittens, cows have calves, ducks have ducklings, and frogs have tadpoles.

5. Animals have physical characteristics that are influenced by changing environmental conditions.

   - Certain animals, such as dogs, get thicker coats in the winter and shed their fur in the summer. Rabbits found in snowy environments have white fur to blend in with their environment, and rabbits found in warmer climates have brown fur to blend in with the earth of their burrows.

6. Animal behavior is also influenced by the conditions of the environment.

   - Some animals, such as birds, build nests in trees to protect themselves from predators.

   - Bears hibernate in the winter after gorging on food in prior months, because their food source is limited in the winter.

   - Birds and fish migrate to different climates in the winter and spring in response to changing temperatures and food sources.

Earth, Weather, and Water

In order to teach about weather and water, teachers should know:

1. The Earth is composed of land, air, and water.

   - There are different characteristics of mountains, rivers, oceans, valleys, deserts and other local land forms.

2. The Earth and its inhabitants—including plants and animals—are affected by changes in weather that occur from day to day and season to season.

   - Weather changes in precipitation and temperature in a particular area daily. There are changes in seasons in certain areas and in other areas the temperature and climate is rather similar throughout the year. These changes influence the growth, development, and behavior of plants and animals as well as the behavior of plants and animals (i.e., certain animals shed fur or hibernate, and leaves fall from the trees).

3. Certain resources from the Earth are used in everyday life, such as water.

   - These resources can be conserved.

   - Water can be conserved by turning off the faucet, collecting rainwater, and using low-flow toilets in houses.

- Energy can be conserved by using compact fluorescent light bulbs, installing solar panels, or waiting before turning on the air conditioner.

In California, children are responsible for a deeper understanding of the Earth and its resources than other states.

First Grade

Properties of Matter

In order to teach about the properties of matter, teachers should know:

1. There are three states of matter: solid, liquid and gas.

   - These states of matter have different properties.

   - Liquids take the shape of their containers but maintain their volume.

   - Air does not have a definite shape or definite volume.

   - Solids have a definite shape and a definite volume.

2. Water evaporates when it is left in an open container at room temperature.

   - Liquid water changes into a gas as it moves into the air.

3. The materials that make up an object determine specific properties.

   - Sinking or floating—some objects made of metal will sink, whereas an object made of wood or plastic floats.

   - Solubility—the amount of an object that can be dissolved in water. A substance that has a high solubility can easily dissolve in water (i.e., salt). A substance that has a low solubility does not dissolve easily in water (i.e., baking soda).

4. Substances mix differently with water.

   - Oil and water do not mix well together, as compared to sugar and water.

5. Observations and measurements of the properties of materials can be made using tools.

   - Hand lenses can help in observing physical characteristics of objects.

   - Rulers can take specific measurements.

   - Thermometers determine how hot or how cold a material is.

   - Balances can determine the weight of an object.

6. Both the properties of objects, as well as the mass of an object, can influence its ability to float.

   - Different materials float better than others (i.e. plastic vs. metal). Think about the design of ships. Originally they were made of wood because it was the substance that floated best. Houseboats built on styrofoam bases float best.

   - Different shapes determine an object's ability to float. A boat floats more safely when its weight is distributed over a larger surface.

   - Children should generally understand boat design.

7. The properties of an object can change when they are placed in different environments.

   - Hot and cold—For example, metals expand when they are heated and contract when they are cooled.

   - Color—Colors can appear differently when they are placed next to each other or on top of each other.

   - Wet and dry—For example, a sponge in a wet environment is dry and small. A sponge in a wet environment absorbs water and increases in size and weight and its shape may even change slightly.

Texas state standards suggest that children should understand that heat from the sun or friction (force opposing the force of an object against another) can cause changes to an object.

Weather and Seasons

In order to teach about the weather and seasons, teachers should know:

1. Different weather conditions occur during the different seasons.

   - There are differences in precipitation, temperature, wind speed, wind direction, cloud cover, cloud types, etc.

   - Weather conditions can be measured, observed, and recorded using weather instruments.

   - Thermometers measure the temperature (how hot or cold it is) in degrees Celsius and degrees Fahrenheit.

   - Anemometers measures the wind speed (wind velocity).

   - Wind vanes measure the direction that the wind is blowing.

   - Rain gauges measure the amount of rain.

- Though weather changes from day to day, trends in temperature and precipitation (rain, snow, sleet and hail) tend to be predictable during different seasons.

2. Temperatures differ in different locations.

  - The temperature inside can be different than the temperature outside.

  - The temperature at night is different than the temperature during the day.

  - The temperature in the shade is different than the temperature in the sun.

3. The position of the sun changes throughout the day.

  - The sun rises in the east and sets in the west. During midday, 12:00 p.m., the sun is directly overhead.

  - The change in the position of the sun is caused by the rotation of the Earth on its imaginary axis during the twenty-four hours of the day. This is the twenty-four-hour-day-and-night cycle.

4. The moon changes appearance over time. The changes of the moon are cyclical and the different shapes are called phases.

  - The shape of the moon that we see results from how much of the moon is visible from the Earth at that point in time.

  - The waxing periods when the moon appears to be getting larger are: new, crescent, first quarter, gibbous.

  - The waning periods when the moon appears to be getting smaller are: full, gibbous, third quarter, crescent.

5. During different times of the day and different months of the year, the position of the sun, stars, and moon change in a predictable pattern due to the rotation of the Earth on its axis (twenty-four-hour cycle) and the revolution of the Earth around the sun (365-day cycle).

  - The sun produces energy, which warms the air, land, and water.

Animal Diversity

In order to teach how animals are alike and different, teachers should know:

1. The body structures of animals have similar and different characteristics.

  - Body coverings of animals—Some animals, like dogs and cats, have fur that helps to regulate heat. Other animals, like fish, have scales that help form a flexible barrier that protects from bumps and blows.

  - Sensory organs of animals—Some animals, like certain types of fish and cats, use whiskers to sense their environment. Many mammals cannot differentiate colors; yet insects can see light in the ultraviolet range, which is outside our spectrum.

- Appendages (attached part of a limb on animals)—These are the wings on a bird, the claws on a crayfish or lobster, etc.

2. There is a relationship between a physical structure and its function.

- Structures can function in obtaining food and water, protection, movement, and support. (For example, the wing of a bird is made up of feathers, hollow bones, muscles, and tendons. Both the shape and the construction of the parts of the wings are designed to help the bird fly.)

3. Certain physical traits of an animal help the animal to survive.

- For example, the shell of a turtle provides protection. The long neck of the giraffe allows the animal to reach high leaves out of the reach of other animals.

4. Animals grow and change in ways that lead them to resemble their parents and other individuals in their species. Some of the characteristics (traits) of animals have been inherited (passed on from generation to generation in the genetic material), such as the number of limbs or the color of coat.

5. Animals have different life cycles and life spans.

California state standards require understanding that both plants and animals need water. Animals require food, whereas plants require light to make their own food. Animals eat plants or other animals for food and may also use plants for shelter and nesting.

California state standards also develop skills of inference by comparing what animals eat with the shape of their teeth. Animals with sharp teeth eat meat, whereas animals with flat teeth eat plants.

Second Grade

Forces and Motion

In order to teach the content of forces and motion, teachers should know:

1. How an object can be described and observed in relation to another object, using words like *over*, *under*, *on top of*, or *next to*.

2. Force is a push or a pull.

- The position or direction of an object can be changed by applying a force: pushing or pulling.

3. Gravity is a force that acts on an object by pulling downward.

- The center of gravity is an imaginary point at which we consider the entire weight of an object to be concentrated. Objects balance on this point. (Think about the Leaning Tower of Pisa. Why has it not fallen? The center of gravity is low enough that the tower is balanced on its base.)

- Gravity also affects objects that travel through air, liquids, and solids.

- Gravity pulls objects down toward the earth.

- Gravity also affects the shape of liquids and solids by helping them to take the shape of the container in which they are kept.

4. Magnets produce a magnetic force that can be used to make objects move together or apart without being forced.

- Depending on the magnetic pull objects can repel or attract each other.

- Certain objects are more magnetic than other objects (i.e., a stainless steel refrigerator versus a piece of plastic).

5. Sound is made by vibrations.

- Vibrations can be described in terms of pitch (frequency of vibrations) and volume (the power of the vibrations).

California state standards require more understanding of forces of motion.

Soil

In order to teach the content of Earth materials, teachers should know:

1. The basic properties and components of soil.

- Soil has living components, such as decaying plant, animal parts (organic matter), and microscopic plants and animals (i.e., bacteria, fungi).

- Soil has nonliving components, such as rocks and minerals.

- Soil also contains water, air, and minerals (inorganic materials).

- Soils can differ in color, texture, capacity to retain water, and ability to support the growth of plants. (For example, some soils are rich in organic materials and can support leafy green plants, while other soils, like those found in the desert, are clay based and support growth of plants with smaller water needs, like cacti.)

2. Erosion is the wearing away and transport of land or soil by the action of wind, water, or ice.

3. Deposition is the process by which wind, water, or ice create and lay down sediment that has been eroded and transported from one area to another one.

   • Erosion and deposition are the result of interactions between air, wind, water, and land.

4. Rocks can be described and categorized in terms of their physical and chemical properties—size, shape, color, and presence of fossils and minerals (e.g., gold and silver).

   • Fossils are the remains of plants and animals that lived years ago. Scientists can study fossil records to learn about the history of the Earth.

   • Smaller rocks are the result of breakage and weathering of larger rocks.

5. Nonliving things, like water, can be naturally occurring.

Texas state standards require knowledge of natural resources such as streams, lakes, and oceans. Texas also requires the identification of how rocks, soil, and water are used and how they can be recycled.

Plant Diversity

In order to teach the content of plant diversity, teachers should know:

1. How to identify and compare the physical structures of a variety of plant parts, including the seeds, leaves, stems, flowers, and roots.

2. Plants grow and change in predictable ways.

   • Plants closely resemble their parents and other individuals of their species.

   • Some of the traits of plants have been inherited, such as the color of the plant and the shape, size, and number of fruit.

3. The life cycle of different plants and their life spans. (See Figure A2.1.)

   • Plants reproduce from seeds, bulbs, and cuttings.

   • Fruits are associated with reproduction of plants.

4. Plants have basic needs in order to survive and thrive, including light, air, water, and nutrients. Nutrients can be gained from the soil.

5. The basic life functions of plants are to grow, take in nutrients, and reproduce.

Figure A 2.1   Life Cycle of a Plant

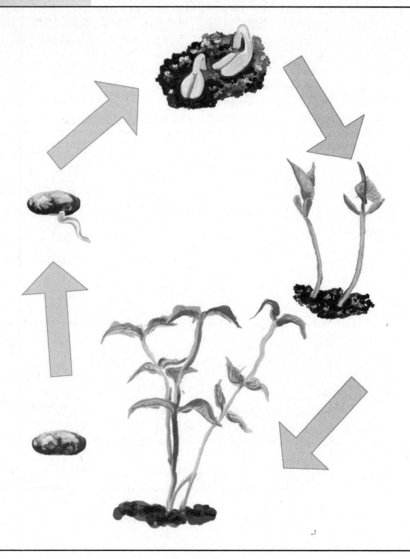

6. Plants, like animals, respond to changes in their environment.

- The leaves of some green plants change position as the direction of the light changes.

- The parts of some plants undergo seasonal changes that enable the plant to grow, seeds to germinate, and leaves to form and grow.

- Plants also respond to gravity and touch.

Life Sciences

In order to teach the content of life sciences, teachers should know:

1. Organisms, including plants and animals, reproduce offspring of their own kind, and the offspring resemble their parents and one another. (For example, geraniums reproduce geraniums.)

2. The sequential stages of life cycles (metamorphosis) are different for different animals.

   - Butterflies produce eggs, which develop into caterpillars, which enter a cocoon stage and emerge as butterflies.

   - Frogs' eggs develop into tadpoles, which gradually lose their tails and develop legs and other characteristics typical of frogs. (See Figure A2.2.)

Figure A 2.2   Life Cycle of a Frog

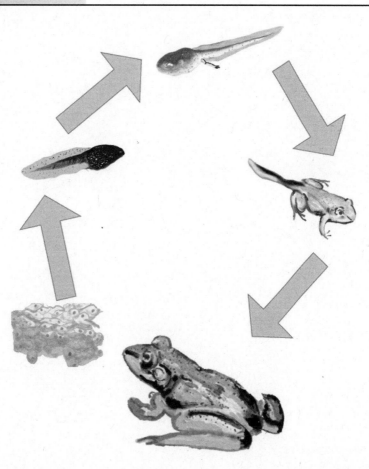

- Organisms such as mice do not experience such morphological (structural/physical) changes.

3. Many characteristics of an organism are inherited from parents, but some characteristics result from adaptations to environment or influenced by the environment.

   - Characteristics that can be environmentally influenced include the weight of an organism, depending on the availability of nutrients. (For example, the length of a goldfish is influenced by the size of the bowl or tank in which it is kept.)

4. There is variation among individuals of one kind of population throughout animal and plant kingdoms. Humans can have different skin tones, hair colors, eye color, and size.

5. Light, gravity, touch, or environmental stress all can have effects on the germination, growth, and development of plants.

6. Flowers and fruits are plant structures that enable the plants to reproduce.

California state standards in second grade discuss the life cycles of both plants and animals.

References

Chapter 1

Gardner, H. (1991). *The unschooled mind: How children think and how schools should teach.* New York: Basic Books.

Gardner, H. (1993). *Creating minds: An anatomy of creativity.* New York: Basic Books.

Gardner, H. (1993). *Frames of mind: The theory of multiple intelligences.* New York: Basic Books.

Gardner, H. (1999). *The disciplined mind: Beyond facts and standardized tests, the K–12 education that every child deserves.* New York: Penguin Putnam.

Gardner, H. (1999). *Intelligence reframed: Multiple intelligences for the 21st century.* New York: Basic Books.

Gardner, H. (2005). *Development and education of mind: The selected works of Howard Gardner.* New York: Routledge.

Gardner, H. (2006). *Multiple intelligences: New horizons in theory and practice.* New York: Basic Books.

Gardner, H. (2007). *Five minds for the future.* Cambridge: Harvard Business School Press.

Koch, J. (2005). *Science stories: Science methods for elementary and middle school teachers,* 3rd ed. New York: Houghton Mifflin.

U.S. Department of Education, Office for Civil Rights, National Center for Education Statistics (NCES), Common Core of Data (CCD). *Public elementary/secondary school universe survey,* 1991–92 to 2005–06. Washington, DC: Author.

Chapter 2

Ahn, W., Gelman, S. A., Amsterlaw, J. A., Hohenstein, J., & Kalish, C. W. (2000). Causal status effects in children's categorization. *Cognition, 76,* 35–43.

Baillargeon, R. (2004). How do infants learn about the physical world? *Current Directions in Psychological Science, 3,* 133–140.

Bar, V., & Travis, A.S. (1991). Children's views concerning phase changes. *Journal of Research in Science Teaching 28*(4), 363–382.

Barab, S. A., & Luehmann, A. L. (2002). Building a sustainable science curriculum: Acknowledging and accommodating local adaptation. *Journal of the Learning Sciences, 10*(4), 320–351.

Barker, M. (1995). A plant is an animal standing on its head. *Journal of Biological Education, 29*(3), 203–208.

Barman, C. R. (1997). Students' views of scientists and science: Results from a national study. *Science and Children, 35*(1), 18–24.

Barman, C. R. (1999). Students' views about scientists and school science: Engaging K–8 teachers in a national study. *Journal of Science Teacher Education, 10*(1), 43–54.

Barman, C., Barman, N., Cox, M. L., Newhouse, K., & Goldston, M. J. (2000). Students' ideas about animals: Results from a national study. *Science and Children, 38*(1) 42–47.

Barman, C. R., Barman, N. S., McNair, S., & Stein, M. (2003). Students' ideas about plants: Results from a national study. *Science and Children*. Retrieved December 1, 2008 from http://proquest.umi.com/pqdlink?did=387219071&Fmt=6&clientId=9269&RQT=309&VName=PQD.

Barman, C., Stein, M., Barman, N., & McNair, S. (2002). Assessing students' ideas about plants. *Science and Children, 10*(1), 25–29.

Bell, B. F. (1981). What is a plant? Some children's ideas. *New Zealand Science Teacher, 31*, 10–14.

Bottomley, L. J., et al. (2001). Lessons learned from the implementation of a GK–12 grant outreach program. Paper presented at the 2001 American Society for Engineering Education Annual Conference, Session 1692.

Brody, M. J. (1993). Student understanding of water and water resources: A review of the literature. Paper presented at the annual meeting of the American Educational Research Association, Atlanta, GA, April. (ERIC Document Reproduction Service No. ED 361 230).

Bullock, M., Gelman, R., & Baillargeon, R. (1982). The development of causal reasoning. In W. J. Friedman (ed.), *The development of psychology of time*. New York: Academic Press.

Cady, J. A., & Rearden, K. (2007). Pre-service teachers' beliefs about knowledge, mathematics and science. *School Science and Mathematics, 107*(6), 237–246.

Carmazza, A., McCloskey, M., & Green, B. (1981). Naïve beliefs in "sophisticated" subjects: Misconceptions about trajectories of objects. *Cognition, 9*, 117–123.

Carey, S. (1991). Knowledge acquisition: Enrichment or conceptual change? In S. Carey & R. Gelman (eds.), *The epigenesist of mind: Essays on biology and cognition* (pp. 257–291). Hillsdale, NJ: Lawrence Erlbaum.

DeLoache, J. S., Pierroutsakos, S. L., & Uttal, D. H. (eds.). (2003). The origins of pictoral competence. *Current Directions in Psychological Science, 12,* 114–118.

Carey, S. (1985). *Conceptual change in childhood.* Cambridge, MA: MIT Press.

Duschl, R. A., Schweingruber, H. A., & Shouse, A. W. (eds.). (2006). *Taking science to school: Learning and teaching science grades K–8.* Committee on Science Learning, Kindergarten Through Eighth Grade. Board on Science Education, Center for Education, Division of Behavioral and Social Science Education. Washington, DC: National Academy Press.

Education Data Partnership. (2007). *School profile: Fiscal year 2005–2006.* Retrieved June 6, 2007, from Education Data Partnership, http://www.ed-data.k12.ca.us/.

Edwards, L., Nabors, M., & Camacho, C. (2002). The dirt on worms. *Science and Children, 40*(1), 42–46.

Erickson, G., & Tiberghien, A. (1985). Heat and temperature. In R. Driver, E. Guesne, & A. Tiberghien (eds.), *Children's ideas in science* (pp. 52–84). London, UK: Open University Press.

Espinoza, F. (2005). Experience conflicts with and undermines instruction and its legacy: Examples from two-dimensional motion. *Physics Education, 40*(3), 274–280.

Ewing, M. S., & Mills, T. J. (1994). Water literacy in college freshman: Could a cognitive imagery strategy improve understanding? *Journal of Environmental Education, 25*(4), 36–40.

Finson, K. (2002). Drawing a scientist: What we do and do not know after fifty years of drawings. *School Science and Mathematics 102*(7), 335–345.

Fraser-Abder, P. (2004). Scientific literacy for all: Are we there yet? In P. Fraser-Abder, *Pedagogical issues in science, mathematics and technology education.* New York Consortium for Professional Development.

Fraser-Abder, P. (2005). Towards scientific literacy for all: An urban science teacher education model. In D. F. Berlin & A. L. White (eds.), *Collaboration for the global improvement of science and mathematics education* (pp. 141–157). Columbus, OH: International Consortium for Research in Science and Mathematics Education.

Gelman, R., & Lucariello, J. (2002). Role of learning in cognitive development. In H. Pashler (series ed.) & R. Gallistel (vol. ed.), *Steven's handbook of experimental psychology: Learning, motivation and emotion* (vol. 3, 3rd ed., pp. 395–443). New York: Wiley.

Greif, M., Nelson, D., Keil, F., & Gutierrez, F. (2006). What do children want to know about animals and artifacts? Domain specific requests for information. *Psychological Science, 17*(6), 455–459.

Harvard-Smithsonian Center for Astrophysics. (1985). *A Private Universe,* video documentary.

Hatano, G., Siegler, R. S., Richards, D. D., Inagaki, K., Stavy, R., & Wax, N. (1993). The development of biological knowledge: A multi-national study. *Cognitive Development, 8,* 47–62.

Henriques, L. (2000). Children's misconceptions about weather: A review of the literature. Retrieved from http://www.csulb.edu/~lhenriqu/NARST2000.htm.

Karplus, R., & Their, H. (1974). *SCIS teacher's handbook.* Berkeley, CA: Science Curriculum Improvement Study.

Keil, F. C. (1983). On the emergence of semantic and conceptual distinctions. *Journal of Experimental Psychology: General, 112,* 357–385.

Koch, J. (1999). *Science stories: Teachers and children as science learners.* Boston: Houghton Mifflin.

Krajcik, J., Blumenfeld, P. C., Marx, R. W., Bass, K. M., & Fredricks, J. (1998). Inquiry in project-based science classrooms: Initial attempts by middle school students. *Journal of the Learning Sciences, 7*(3/4), 313–350.

Krist, H., Fieberg, E. L., & Wilkening, F. (1993). Intuitive physics in action and judgment: The development and knowledge about projectile motion. *Journal of Experimental Psychology: Learning Memory and Cognition, 19*(4), 952–966.

Lee, O., Eichinger, D. C., Anderson, C. W., Berkheimer, G. D., & Blakeslee, T. D. (1993). Changing middle school students' conceptions of matter and molecules. *Journal of Research in Science Teaching, 30*(3), 249–270.

McDuffie, Jr., T. E. (2001). Scientists—geeks and nerds? Dispelling teachers' stereotypes of scientists. *Science and Children* (May), 16–19.

McNair, S., & Stein, M. (2001). Drawing on their understanding: Using illustrations to invoke deeper thinking about plants. Paper presented at the Association for the Education of Teachers of Science Annual Meeting, Costa Mesa, CA.

National Research Council (NRC). (1996). *National science education standards.* Washington, DC: National Academy Press.

Office of the Press Secretary. (2002). *Fact sheet: No child left behind act.* Retrieved August 8, 2007, from www.whitehouse.gov/news/releases/2002/01/20020108.html.

Osborne, R. J., & Cosgrove, M. (1983). Children's conceptions of the changes of state of water. *Journal of Research I: Science Teaching, 20*(9), 825–838.

Osborne, R. J., & Freyberg, P. (1985). *Learning in Science*. London: Heinemann.

Philips, W. C. (1991). Earth science misconceptions. *Science Teacher, 58*(2), 21–23.

Poulin-Dubois, D., & Rakison, D. H. (2001). Developmental origin of the animate-inanimate distinction. *Psychological Bulletin, 127*(2), 209–228.

Rahm, J., & Charbonneau, P. (1997). Probing stereotypes through students' drawings of scientists. *American Journal of Physics, 65*(8), 774–778.

Rastovac, J. J. & Slavsky, D. B. (1986). The use of paradoxes as an instructional strategy. *Journal of College Science Teaching, 16*(2), 113–118.

Richards, D. D., & Siegler, R. S. (1984). The effects of task requirements on children's life judgments. *Child Development, 55,* 1687–1696.

Richards, D. D., & Siegler, R. S. (1986). Children's understandings of the attributes of life. *Journal of Experimental Child Psychology, 42,* 1–22.

Roth, K. (1985). *Food for plants: Teacher's guide*. Research series no. 153. East Lansing: Michigan State University, Institute of Research on Teaching. (ERIC Document Reproduction Services No. ED # 256 624).

Ryman, D. (1974). Children's understanding of the classification of living organisms. *Journal of Biological Education, 8,* 140–144.

Schoon, K. J. (1989). Misconceptions in the earth sciences: A cross-age study. Paper presented at the annual meeting of the National Associations for Research in Science Teaching, San Francisco, CA. (ERIC Document Reproduction Service No. ED 306 076).

Schoon, K. (1995). The origin and extent of alternative conceptions in the earth and space sciences: A survey of pre-service elementary teachers. *Journal of Elementary Science Education, 7*(2), 27–46.

Sere, M. G. (1985). The gaseous state, in R. Driver, E. Guesne, & A. Tiberghien (eds.), *Children's ideas in science* (pp. 105–123). London, UK: Open University Press.

Shanon, B. (1976). Aristotelianism, Newtownianism and the physics of the layman. *Perceptions, 5,* 241–243.

Smith, E. L., & Anderson, C. W. (1984). Plants as producers: A case study of elementary science teaching. *Journal of Research in Science Teaching, 21,* 685–698.

Sjøberg, S. (2000). *Science and scientists: The SAS-study. Cross-cultural evidence and perspectives on pupils' interests, experiences and perceptions*. University of Oslo.

Stavy, R. (1991). Children's ideas about matter. *School Science and Mathematics, 91*(6), 240–244.

Stavy, R., & Wax, N. (1989). Children's conceptions of plants as living things. *Human Development, 62,* 767–781.

Stein, M., & McNair, S. (2002). Science drawings as a tool for analyzing conceptual understanding. Paper presented at the Association for the Education of Teachers of Science Annual Meeting, Charlotte, NC.

Stepans, J. (1985). Biology in elementary schools: Children conceptions of life. *American Biology Teacher, 47*(4), 222–225.

Stepans, J. (1994). *Targeting students' science misconceptions.* Riverview, FL: Idea Factory.

Science Accountability Act (H.R. 35). Retrieved from http://www.govtrack.us/congress/bill.xpd?bill=h110-35.

Tunnicliffe, S. D., & Reiss, M. J. (2000). Building a model of the environment: How do children see plants? *Journal of Biological Education, 34*(4), 172–177.

Watts, M. (1983). Some alternative views of energy. *Physics Education, 18,* 213–216.

Wellman, H. M. (1990). *The child's theory of mind.* Cambridge, MA: MIT Press.

Yoachim, C. M., & Meltzoff, A. N. (2003, October). *Cause and effect in the mind of the preschool child.* Poster presented at the biennial meeting of the Cognitive Development Society, Park City, UT.

Chapter 3

Byrnes, D. A., & Kiger, G. (eds.). (2005). *Common bonds: Anti-bias teaching in a diverse society.* Olney, MD: Association for Childhood Education International.

Grayson, D., & Martin, M. (2006) *Generating expectations for student achievement: An equitable approach to educational excellence.* Gray Mill, CA: Canyon Lake.

Chapter 4

Bybee, R. W., Taylor, J. A., Gardner, A., Van Scotter, P., Powell, J. A., & Westbrook, A., et al. (2006). The BSCS 5E instructional model: Origins, effectiveness and applications. In *Executive Summary.* Retrieved August 8, 2007, from http://www.bscs.org/library/BSCS_5E_Model_Executive_Summary2006.pdf.

Barab, S. A., & Luehmann, A. L. (2002). Building sustainable science curriculum: Acknowledging and accommodating local adaptation. *Journal of the Learning Sciences, 10*(4), 320–351.

Koch, J. (1999). *Science stories: Teachers and children as science learners.* Boston: Houghton Mifflin.

Krajcik, J., Blumenfeld, P. C., Marx, R. W., Bass, K. M., & Fredricks, J. (1998). Inquiry in project-based science classrooms: Initial attempts by middle school students. *Journal of the Learning Sciences, 7*(3/4), 313–350.

National Research Council (NRC). 1996. *National science education standards.* Washington, DC: National Academy Press.

Prince, M., & Felder, R. (2007). The many faces of inductive teaching and learning. *Journal of College Science Teaching, 36*(5), 14–20.

Chapter 5

Harlen, W. (1999). Purposes and procedures for assessing science process skills. Assessment in education: Principles, policy and practice, 6(1), 129–144. Retrieved June 11, 2009, from http://www.informaworld.com/10.1080/09695949993044.

Harlen, W. (2001). *Primary science: Taking the plunge.* Portsmouth: Heinemann.

Harlen, W. (2005). *Teaching, learning and assessing science 5–12.* Thousand Oaks: Sage.

Chapter 6

National Research Council (NRC). (1996). *National science education standards.* Washington, DC: National Academy Press.

Koch, J. (1999). *Science stories: Teachers and children as science learners.* Boston: Houghton Mifflin.

Chapter 7

Grant, T., & Littlejohn, G. (2005). *Teaching green: The elementary years.* Gabriola: New Society Publishers.

Leslie, C. W. (2005). *Into the field: A guide to locally focused teaching.* Great Barrington: Orion Society.

Moyer, R. H., Hackett, J. K., & Everett, S. A. (2006). *Teaching science as investigations: Modeling inquiry through learning cycle lessons.* Upper Saddle River: Prentice Hall.

Russell, H. R. (1998). *Ten minute field trips: Using the school grounds for environmental studies.* Arlington: National Science Teachers Association.

Education Programs

This list consists of selected education programs for use in field trips. Many of these sites also conduct virtual field trips. You should also visit the following Website for links to additional programs: http://www.yallaa.com/directory/Reference/Museums/Science

Agropolis-Museum—Science Center dealing with topics such as food, nutrition, agriculture, with a historical approach on a worldwide scale. Montpellier, France.

Arizona Science Center—Planetarium, hands-on learning exhibits and IMAX theatre. Phoenix, Arizona.

Canada Science and Technology Museum—Features educational activities, online exhibits, and museum events. Located in Ontario, Ottawa.

The Franklin Institute Science Museum—Take a virtual tour or find out about events, exhibits, and membership. Located in Philadelphia, Pennsylvania.

Liberty Science Center—Science museum in New Jersey. Explore LSC's three themed floors: Environment, Health, and Invention, featuring dozens of exciting hands-on exhibits.

Mid America Science Museum—Offers interactive exhibits that explore such subjects as perception, energy, sound, light and gravity. Visitors can fly a hot-air balloon, generate electricity, see a laser light show or walk along nature trails. Includes brief history of museum, hours, admission rates and directions. Located in Hot Springs, Arkansas.

Museum of Science and Industry—Features a coal mine, a U-505 submarine, intelligent LEGO bricks, and travel through virtual reality. Located in Chicago, Illinois.

NYSCI—Exhibits, often interactive, on sound, light, atoms, microbes, AIDS, astronomy. Includes a science playground. Considered one of the top ten science museums in the country. Located in Queens, New York.

Omniplex Science Museum—Offers a diverse collection of interactive and historic exhibits and programs. Located in Oklahoma City.

Science Museum of Virginia—Learning tools, educational resources for kids and grown-ups with links to museums in Richmond and around Virginia.

Smithsonian National Air and Space Museum—Features 23 main exhibition galleries, each displaying major artifacts from the Museum's collection. Located in Washington, DC.

Chapter 8

Victor, E., & Kellough, R. D. (2000). *Science for the elementary and middle school,* 9th ed. New York: Merrill/Prentice Hall.

Koch, J. (2005). *Science stories: Science methods for elementary and middle school teachers,* 3rd ed. New York: Houghton Mifflin.

Appendix 1

National Research Council (NCR). (1996). *National science education standards.* Washington, DC: National Academy Press.

American Association for the Advancement of Science (AAAS). (1993). *Project 2061: Benchmarks for science literacy: A tool for curriculum reform.* New York: Oxford University Press.

New York City Department of Education (NYC DOE). (2007). NYC science scope and sequence. *NYC DOE curriculum and professional development: Mathematics and science.* Retrieved June 6, 2007, from http://schools.nyc.gov/NR/rdonlyres/C17923F6-91D9-4B19-AC89-B96160F12F99/24139/K8SSScience1.pdf.

Appendix 2

American Association for the Advancement of Science. (2001). *Project 2061: Atlas of science literacy.* Washington, DC: National Science Teachers Association.

American Association for the Advancement of Science. (2007). *Project 2061: Atlas of science literacy,* vol. 2. Washington, DC: National Science Teachers Association.

Index

Notes

Notes

Notes

Notes

Notes

Notes

Notes

Notes

Notes

Notes